TRAINING FOR PROFIT

DATE DUE

DEMCO 38-297

Latest titles in the McGraw-Hill Training Series

DESIGNING AND ACHIEVING COMPETENCY
A Competency-Based Approach to Developing People and
Organizations
Editors: Rosemary Boam
and Paul Sparrow   ISBN 0-07-707572-2

TOTAL QUALITY TRAINING
The Quality Culture and Quality Trainer
Brian Thomas   ISBN 0-07-707472-6

CAREER DEVELOPMENT AND PLANNING
A Guide for Managers, Trainers and Personnel Staff
Malcolm Peel   ISBN 0-07-707554-4

SALES TRAINING
A Guide to Developing Effective Salespeople
Frank S. Salisbury   ISBN 0-07-707458-0

CLIENT-CENTRED CONSULTING
A Practical Guide for Internal Advisers and Trainers
Peter Cockman, Bill Evans
and Peter Reynolds   ISBN 0-07-707685-0

TRAINING TO MEET THE TECHNOLOGY CHALLENGE
Trevor Bentley   ISBN 0-07-707589-7

IMAGINATIVE EVENTS
A Sourcebook of Innovative Simulations, Exercises, Puzzles and Games
Ken Jones   ISBN 0-07-707679-6 Volume I
        ISBN 0-07-707680-X Volume II
        ISBN 0-07-707681-8 for set of Volumes I & II

LEARNING THROUGH SIMULATIONS
A Guide to the Design and Use of Simulations in Business and Education
John Fripp   ISBN 0-07-707588-9

MEETINGS MANUAL
A Manual of Effective Training Material
Leslie Rae   ISBN 0-07-707782-2

WORKSHOPS THAT WORK
100 Ideas to Make Your Training Events More Effective
Tom Bourner, Phil Race
and Vivien Martin   ISBN 0-07-707800-4

Details of these and other titles in the series are available from:

The Product Manager, Professional Books, McGraw-Hill Book Company Europe,
Shoppenhangers Road, Maidenhead, Berkshire, SL6 2QL, United Kingdom.
Telephone: 0628 23432. Fax: 0628 770224

Training for Profit

A guide to the integration of training in an organization's success

Philip Darling

McGRAW-HILL BOOK COMPANY

London · New York · St Louis · San Francisco · Auckland
Bogotá · Caracas · Lisbon · Madrid · Mexico · Milan
Montreal · New Delhi · Panama · Paris · San Juan · São Paulo
Singapore · Sydney · Tokyo · Toronto

Published by
McGRAW-HILL Book Company Europe
Shoppenhangers Road, Maidenhead, Berkshire, SL6 2QL, England
Telephone: 0628 23432
Fax: 0628 770224

British Library Cataloguing in Publication Data
Darling, Philip
  Training for Profit: Guide to the Integration of Training in an Organization's
  Success. – 2 Rev. ed. – (McGraw-Hill Training Series)
  I. Title II. Series
  658. 3124

ISBN 0-07-707786-5

Library of Congress Cataloging-in-Publication Data
Darling, Philip
    Training for profit: a guide to the integration of training in an
  organization's success/Philip Darling.
      p.   cm.—(The McGraw-Hill training series)
    Includes bibliographical references and index.
    ISBN 0-07-707786-5
    1. Employees—Training of.   2. Training needs.   3. Employee
  training personnel—Training of.   4. Strategic planning.   5. Success
  in business.   I. Title   II. Series
  HF5549.5.T7D36   1993
  658.3'124—dc20   93-2921
                                                                        CIP

12345 CL 96543

Typeset by Book Ens Limited, Baldock, Herts
Printed and bound in Great Britain by Clays Ltd, St Ives plc

Contents

Series preface

Training and development are now firmly centre stage in most organizations, if not all. Nothing unusual in that—for some organizations. They have always seen training and development as part of the heart of their businesses—but more and more must see it that same way.

The demographic trends through the 1990s will inject into the marketplace severe competition for good people who will need good training. Young people without conventional qualifications, skilled workers in redundant crafts, people out of work, women wishing to return to work—all will require excellent training to fit them to meet the job demands of the 1990s and beyond.

But excellent training does not spring from what we have done well in the past. T&D specialists are in a new ball game. 'Maintenance' training—training to keep up skill levels to do what we have always done—will be less in demand. Rather, organization, work and market change training are now much more important and will remain so for some time. Changing organizations and people is no easy task, requiring special skills and expertise which, sadly, many T&D specialists do not possess.

To work as a 'change' specialist requires us to get to centre stage—to the heart of the company's business. This means we have to ask about future goals and strategies and even be involved in their development, at least as far as T&D policies are concerned.

This demands excellent communication skills, political expertise, negotiating ability, diagnostic skills—indeed, all the skills a good internal consultant requires.

The implications for T&D specialists are considerable. It is not enough merely to be skilled in the basics of training, we must also begin to act like business people and to think in business terms and talk the language of business. We must be able to resource training not just from within but by using the vast array of external resources. We must be able to manage our activities as well as any other manager. We must share in the creation and communication of the company's vision. We must never let the goals of the company out of our sight.

In short, we may have to grow and change with the business. It will be hard. We shall have to demonstrate not only relevance but also value for money and achievement of results. We shall be our own boss, as accountable for results as any other line manager, and we shall have to deal with fewer internal resources.

The challenge is on, as many T&D specialists have demonstrated to me over the past few years. We need to be capable of meeting that challenge. This is why McGraw-Hill Book Company Europe have planned and launched this major new training series—to help us meet that challenge.

The series covers all aspects of T&D and provides the knowledge base from which we can develop plans to meet the challenge. They are practical books for the professional person. They are a starting point for planning our journey into the twenty-first century.

Use them well. Don't just read them. Highlight key ideas, thoughts, action pointers or whatever, and have a go at doing something with them. Through experimentation we evolve; through stagnation we die.

I know that all the authors in the McGraw-Hill Training Series would want me to wish you good luck. Have a great journey into the twenty-first century.

ROGER BENNETT
Series Editor

About the series editor

Roger Bennett has over 20 years' experience in training, management education, research and consulting. He has long been involved with trainer training and trainer effectiveness. He has carried out research into trainer effectiveness and conducted workshops, seminars and conferences on the subject around the world. He has written extensively on the subject including the book *Improving Trainer Effectiveness* (Gower). His work has taken him all over the world and has involved directors of companies as well as managers and trainers.

Roger Bennett has worked in engineering, several business schools (including the International Management Centre, where he launched the UK's first masters degree in T&D) and has been a board director of two companies. He is the editor of the *Journal of European Industrial Training* and was series editor of the ITD's *Get In There* workbook and video package for the managers of training departments. He now runs his own business called The Management Development Consultancy.

Acknowledgements

I would like to thank Gordon Brand, David Cottier, Jill Darling, Dave Francis, John Elliott, Jean Hay-Burns and David Parton for their help in the preparation of this book. Their perceptions and the quality of their advice has made a great difference.

I am also grateful to the authors and publishers who have given permission to draw from their published work.

Introduction

The long-term success or failure of any firm depends upon the quality of its workforce. Providing the right sort of training and development, and encouraging people to take advantage of it, will not only foster that quality but will also give the organization its most basic and central source of competitive advantage—the skills to do the job well.

But in practical terms, how can the contribution made by training be assessed? How can appropriate and effective training strategies and plans be developed? And how can appropriate levels of training investment be determined?

Training for Profit presents the essential concepts, frameworks and basic tools to develop training strategies and plans relevant to the needs of a business. Moreover, it promises a powerful approach, which can greatly enhance the trainer's credibility within the organization by building a bridge between the language of business and the language of training.

By applying well-proven techniques drawn from the disciplines of corporate strategy, organization analysis and financial appraisal to a training perspective, the book aims to guide the trainer through the process of:

- Understanding the contribution of people and training to the business
- Relating training to the objectives and competitive strategy of the organization
- Understanding the elements of costs and their significance in identifying training needs and opportunities
- Using the techniques of contribution analysis as a basis for determining training strategy
- Relating training specifically to the needs of a business to improve and sustain levels of profitability and financial performance
- Evaluating and formulating training priorities in the different functions of the business
- Developing a framework for implementation

Today's twin problems of an increasingly competitive business environment and demographic change have done much to heighten awareness of the importance of training as a means of achieving organization effectiveness. Yet few organizations are aware of their direct costs of training and even fewer appreciate the opportunities that are missed.

Training for Profit offers a systematic way of examining the activities of an organization in order to analyse training needs and opportunities and their potential contributions to its overall effectiveness and profitability. It is drawn from my experience of working in large and small companies spanning the engineering and food and drink industries and, more recently, from my research and teaching experience in the broad area of manpower studies and particular interest in human resource development.

I hope that managers and trainers who are looking for guidelines to develop sound training strategies and plans will find this approach a helpful and stimulating starting point. The book is organized in six parts.

Part One examines the importance of assessing training needs and pre-paring training plans. It also presents a general framework for analysing an organization in order to identify its training needs and introduces the conceptual foundations of the Training for Profit approach.

Parts Two and Three provide a set of analytical tools to help the trainer understand the business and assess training needs, opportunities and priorities. They enable the trainer to form an overview of the organization in terms of its strategy, structure and culture and to understand its per-formance and potential in measurable and financial terms. They are drawn from authoritative sources whose articulation of fundamental approaches to business planning, organization and financial analysis represent landmarks for the trainer. Those with responsibility for training—whether line managers or personnel and training professionals—need to appreciate the potential contribution of these ideas to the development of relevant and coherent training plans.

Part Four focuses on factors to be taken into account in establishing a framework for action, and reviews the role and skills of the trainer in managing the process of conducting the assessment of training needs and planning how best to meet them.

Part Five provides a comprehensive case study reflecting the application of the Training for Profit approach in action. It shows how training strategies and plans can be developed to strike an appropriate balance between the achievement of improvements in performance in the short term and, in the longer term, the development of organizational effectiveness.

Part Six returns to the broader perspective and discusses a range of contemporary issues for consideration in assessing the overall training needs of an organization.

The appendices provide a brief review of financial statements and an *aide-mémoire* designed to assist in the process of reviewing an organization's strategy and performance as a whole, as a basis for identifying key areas where training can contribute to improving performance.

The reader can use this book in a number of ways. First, in larger companies, general and line managers with responsibility for training, either across their organization or within particular functions of it, are likely to find it helpful in clarifying their understanding of the potential contribution training can make to a business. Trainers in these companies are already likely to be aware of the effect that such factors as strategy, structure and culture can have on performance, but may have difficulty in developing profitable training strategies and demonstrating their worth. For this group, therefore, the book should provide an analytical tool.

In medium- and smaller-sized companies, where perhaps responsibilities for training and the assessment of training needs are not so clearly defined, the reader may gain most by having an understanding of the entire framework as a basis for addressing the training needs of his or her function or organization. For others (for example, consultants) it can be used as both an intervention strategy and a tool for evaluating training systems and effectiveness.

Finally, this book is written for practitioners—whether managers or trainers, consultants, management advisers, teachers or students of personnel, training and management—and others, such as civil servants or members of Training and Enterprise Councils, seeking to understand the business context of training in order to formulate relevant policies.

Each will draw something different from it, so that finding the right term to embrace all these groups is difficult. In using the word 'trainer' throughout, I hope that each group will recognize their common interest. I also hope that acknowledging the very wide range of activities which can fall within the trainer's scope and responsibility will contribute to a wider understanding of the potential of the trainer's role and greater acceptance and recognition of its importance and value.

To Josh

PART ONE

The overall assessment of training needs

Introduction

An environment in which organizations are increasingly under pressure to compete requires a shift in thinking from everyone. Many organizations need to increase significantly their investment in training to cope with these pressures. If they don't, they risk sabotaging their own efforts to achieve their objectives. In contrast, organizations which not only invest in training but also direct it towards developing overall effectiveness enhance their capacity to survive. For trainers this means a change in emphasis from their traditional orientation towards identifying individual training needs and supervision of training programmes in favour of a much more business-oriented approach aimed at improving their organization's total performance.

But how can trainers contribute to developing overall organization effectiveness? And, even more importantly, how can they demonstrate the value of their contribution?

The first part of this book shows a context in which these questions can be addressed. Chapter 1 provides a setting by examining the need for the overall assessment of training needs as a basis for planning training to meet the needs of the business. In the process it looks at not just the consequences of not adopting a systematic approach but also at some of the barriers to doing so.

Chapter 2 sets out the conceptual foundations underlying the Training for Profit approach and provides an overview of its application and the process involved. In doing so, it provides the framework for the rest of the book.

1 The overall assessment and planning of training needs—the key to profitable training

The setting

The central theme of this book is that for most organizations there is no more important task than that of developing their workforces and creating conditions which encourage the greatest use of individual abilities. In short, the long-term success or failure of a business depends upon the quality of its workforce in general and its skills in particular. Only through the possession and development of skills, both individually and collectively, will an organization be able to maintain and develop its most central source of added value and competitive advantage.

This is already apparent in those organizations which have recognized the need to increase their investment in training to cope with the changing competitive pressures and developments in the labour market. Such organizations are aware that if they do not make this investment, they risk sabotaging their own efforts to achieve their objectives and their capacity to survive.

Indeed, the financial structure of many businesses, probably the majority, and the threats they consequently face implies that most organizations need to have an over-riding objective to achieve an improved return on their assets. Until this is done, there is probably little point in trying to do anything else. In the process, these organizations will need to develop the ability to learn more effectively than hitherto. Only by doing so will they be able to create a sustainable business.

This setting provides many opportunities for those with the ability to think and to act. In particular, for trainers, there is tremendous scope to apply their skills directly towards improving organizational performance.

The issues for trainers

In order to show their worth, trainers need to be able to carry out a proper assessment of training needs. The importance of this is increasingly apparent from both empirical and theoretical research. This shows:

- High-performing firms to be more systematic in their approach to human resource management (HRM) practices than low-performing firms

- A strong positive relationship between financial performance and the degree of integration between HRM and corporate strategy.[1]

To carry out a full assessment of training needs, trainers, besides their professional skills, must have a broad base of business knowledge and familiarity with the basic concepts, approaches and tools of business planning. Only by doing so will they be able to make the connection between the future needs of the business and the people involved, while at the same time retaining and building their credibility with line management.

Such issues raise the question as to the extent to which managements in general, and trainers in particular, possess the ability to identify their organization's need for skills as a basis for developing appropriate training strategies. Unfortunately, research findings in this area are far from encouraging. For example, the *Skill Needs in Britain Report*, commissioned by the Training Agency and covering a population of more than 143 000 establishments employing more than 25 staff across all industrial sectors excluding Agriculture, Forestry and Fishing, found that:

1 Fewer than 48 per cent of firms had formal business plans.
2 Fewer than 35 per cent had formal manpower plans.
3 Fewer than 41 per cent had formal training plans.[2]

More recent still, research carried out for IBM and covering nearly 3000 respondents worldwide highlighted the need for human resource executives to shift from an operational to a strategic role and the huge gap between current and desired performance.[3]

Consistent with much other research, these surveys confirm that business planning is the preserve of sales, marketing and finance departments. Along with information technology and the personnel function, training tends to be the least called upon to get involved in the planning process, despite the acknowledgement of these companies that human resource issues are critical to their success.

This raises again the spectre of the vicious circle highlighted by Karen Legge in the 1970s in which the personnel function as a whole, by being limited to day-to-day matters, tends to become overtaken by firefighting activities. Besides being able to provide too little assistance, too late, the personnel function's image of limited capability to help is confirmed resulting in its continued exclusion from the planning process (Legge, 1978).

Applying the analogy to training, it is easy to see why the activities of many trainers tend to be limited to meeting the training needs of individual employees, rather than contributing to the strategic development of the organization. Being so limited, they are in turn unable to acquire the knowledge, experience and skills necessary to contribute to overall business performance. In consequence, the view that trainers lack business understanding and the real ability to support the business is confirmed.

The important conclusions to be drawn underline the extent to which in any organization:

1 Senior management need to recognize and accept their overall responsibility for training.
2 Line managers need to possess awareness and understanding of the training function, so as to formulate clear expectations of its role and contribution and fulfil their own direct responsibility for it.
3 Business plans are necessary as a basis for assessing training needs.
4 Training investment needs to be directed towards, and integrated with, the needs of the business.
5 Trainers need to have the capacity to contribute fully to the development of the organization and its workforce at a strategic level.

The consequences of inadequate training needs assessment

If organizations fail to understand the training contribution and relate training to the needs of the business it is probable that they will experience skill shortages and deficiencies. In specific terms, failure to do so can be expected to contribute to:

- Loss of business
- Constraints on business development
- Higher labour turnover
- Poorer-quality applicants
- Increased overtime working
- Higher rates of pay, overtime premiums and supplements
- Higher recruitment costs, including advertising, time and incentives
- Greater pressure and stress on management and staff to provide cover
- Pressure on job-evaluation schemes, grading structures, payment systems and career structures
- Additional retention costs in the form of flexible working time, job-sharing, part-time working, shift-working, etc.
- Needs for job redesign and revision of job specifications
- Undermining career paths and structures
- Higher training costs

Assessing the extent of such problems is notoriously difficult, not least because of changes in the economic environment. However, at the peak of the economic cycle it is usual for the large majority of organizations to report problems of recruitment and retention. Even in recession many organizations:

1 Find it difficult to recruit enough people with the right mix of skills and experience to fill a wide range of jobs,
2 Report a 'significant gap' between the skills their workforces possess and those needed to meet the business objectives,
3 Experience severe restrictions to business development or lose business as a result,
4 Encounter additional running or high recruitment costs.[4]

Some implications

Albeit a highly uncomfortable analysis, the current state of play suggests that many managers and trainers may be too unskilled to recognize their own need for skills—let alone those of the organizations for which they work—and that this lack of recognition is symptomatic of the problem itself. This is reflected in the low status of the training function in many organizations and the widespread lack of consideration of training issues in the corporate planning process.

In many ways such problems are merely indicative of the tip of an iceberg. Underlying them may be issues of management style, structure, information—or lack of it—all pointing to inappropriate attitudes, knowledge and skills and the need for training. Failure to address them leads almost inevitably to the deterioration of an organization's operating performance, erosion of its capital base and, ultimately, its demise.

More than this, it would seem that very few organizations can claim to have a high concern for strategy and a consistent and integrated approach to training. Thus recognition of the need to invest in people and develop 'human capital'—as distinct from a short-term approach aimed at getting the right people in the right place at the right time—would seem to be light-years away.

The need for planning

It is self-evident that developing and making the best use of resources requires careful planning. However, in trying to understand the evident reluctance of many organizations to do so, one could point to the traditional objections raised by those who don't, won't or can't plan.

These are likely to be centred round such themes as it's too time consuming, involves too much work, requires information not available, or that the future is too uncertain. However, such objections fly in the face of evidence of those organizations using planning, not just for the purpose of maintaining the business and developing their competitiveness but also for developing planning skills *per se*.

Although the absence of business planning does not make planning for training impossible, it does make it less systematic and much more difficult and speculative. Also, almost certainly, it reflects the need for training of both functional specialists and line management in understanding the planning process and skills in its application.

More than this, whatever the reasons for lack of planning, the widespread extent of the problem carries important implications for the way not just trainers are trained but also, at least as importantly, those in line management. Without such training an organization's needs for skills and their appropriate management are unlikely to be met.

Planning for skills

It is within the context of planning that organizations can begin to gauge the skills gaps that confront them. Such gaps may be either:

Quantitative—for example, relating to specific occupations as a result of technological change outpacing education and training provision, or *Qualitative*—for example, where an organization lacks appropriate skills to maintain and develop its performance in line with its needs and aspirations.

Additionally, in the sense that almost all resources, and especially the skills of the workforce, involve elements of cost, they can be seen to be scarce. In consequence, any increase in the output of one product or service can only be achieved at the expense or opportunity cost of another. Thus, whatever its objectives, every organization needs to decide how best to allocate its resources and skills in order to optimize its productive capacity.

This is, of course, the crux of the matter, especially for those organizations where productivity falls short of that of their competitors. Such organizations often see skill gaps and shortages—if they see them at all—in terms of quantitative aspects (for example, the shortage of school leavers, nurses, engineers, IT specialists or foreign-exchange dealers) rather than the deeper and fundamentally more important qualitative issues.

These qualitative issues are crucial. For example, Rosabeth Moss Kanter, editor of *Harvard Business Review*, reckons that rapid change in the business environment is resulting in a form of corporate Olympics in which every element is in motion—technology, suppliers, customers, employees, corporate structure, industry structure, government regulation—and none of this can be counted on to remain stable for very long (Kanter, 1989).

In this contest Kanter maintains that it is impossible to win by using the old corporate forms. Instead, in what she terms the four F's, organizations need to be Focused, Fast, Friendly and Flexible. To achieve this, she argues that management needs to give priority to 'ensuring that people at all levels are able to concentrate on doing what they do best, in a company itself fully focused on maximizing its core business competence' (p. 344, 1989). The underlying imperative is to ensure that all activities add value, allowing the company to do 'more with less'.

The danger in this is that, unless it is skilfully planned and managed, the restructuring process implied may result in subtracting value rather than adding it. Kanter suggests that this is particularly likely to happen where poor management overestimates the level of cooperation it will get and underestimates the transition costs.

The resulting side-effects all tend to reduce productivity. In turn, there follows a loss of energy, resources and initiative culminating in a diminution of confidence in management and, for many, an increasing sense of powerlessness and lack of control over their individual fate. In due course this manifests itself in a loss of commitment.

These qualitative issues are considered in an even sharper context by

Richard Tanner Pascale (1990) in his analysis of how successful companies stay ahead. In doing so, he shows just how crucial and subtle they can be when he observes:

Nothing fails like success. Winning organizations—whether the Israeli Army, the U.S. Olympic Committee in its heyday, expanding young enterprises or established global corporations—are locked into a deadly paradox. This is because great strengths are inevitably the root of weakness. Organizations have a tendency to do what they best know how to do; they are, if you will, the ultimate conservatives. Couple this with the tendency of dedicated and energetic leadership to drive an organization to be still better at what it already does well, and we propel ourselves on a trajectory toward excess. Results may be positive and profitable in the short run, but excesses are fatal over time. The golden adage 'Stick to your knitting' becomes an epitaph. This is because our fixation on 'what is' obscures that other aggravating necessity of worrying about 'what isn't' and what 'might be' (p. 11).

In the process, Pascale reflects the importance of organizational learning to ensure understanding and the capacity to cope with the sorts and nature of challenges facing organizations not just in the present but also in the future. Only by doing so will it be possible to balance and integrate the needs of the organization and its members with the demands of the environment. At the same time, it should be apparent that for most organizations there will not be a single, neat or permanent solution.

The need for balance

From a training perspective this reflects the need to balance the organization's requirement for basic and on-going training systems on the one hand, while also providing for its needs to adapt to changes in the environment, on the other. In this sense, training can be seen as the common denominator and vital not just to meet new and changing demands but also to produce innovation. At the same time, training and development is also the key to meeting the needs of employees whose traditional notion of property rights attaching to a particular job or career are increasingly under threat.

Seeking to achieve this balance underlines the role and importance of training in bringing together and underpinning all the activities of the organization. Thus, whereas the cost of not planning for such needs can be very high, organizations which plan their training are in a position to:

- Upgrade skills continuously
- Improve performance
- Enable people to be redeployed, thereby avoiding layoffs and redundancies, following, for example, changes in strategy, structure, technology or market conditions
- Help people to re-enter the labour market when continued employment or career development can no longer be offered
- Attract the most suitable people into the organization
- Provide potential for promotions and flexibility

- Improve organizational competitiveness
- Develop their human capital

In the process, the real pay-off for the company is that its investment in training will produce a committed, talented and results-oriented workforce with the skills to create added value and develop the business.

Notes

1 See, for example, Dr Stephen Fox, Morgan Tanton and Professor Stuart McCleay, 'Human resource management, corporate strategy and financial performance', The Management School, Lancaster University, April 1992. Carried out as part of the ESRC's 'Competitiveness and Regeneration of British Industry' initiative.
2 IFF Research 1990.
3 Carried out by Towers Perrin and reported in *Personnel Management*, May 1992, p.3.
4 An indication of the size of the problem is given in the Training Agency survey. See also *Recruitment and Retention: Tackling the Universal Problem*, IRS Employment Trends No. 447, 6 September 1989.

References

Kanter, R.M. (1989) *When Giants Learn to Dance*, New York: Simon & Schuster.

Legge, K. (1978) *Power, Innovation, and Problem-solving in Personnel Management*, New York: McGraw-Hill, p.56.

Pascale, R.T. (1990) *Managing on the Edge: how successful companies use conflict to stay ahead*, Harmondsworth: Viking, p.11.

2 Assessing company training needs—the Training for Profit approach

Conceptual foundations

The Training for Profit approach maintains that skills are the basic and central source of an organization's effectiveness. Even more importantly, it holds that further investigation of a 'profit gap' or other shortfall in performance will almost certainly reveal a 'skill gap'. By extension:

Profit gap = performance gap = skill gap = training gap

The process of bridging this gap requires consistent and integrated training strategies directed towards continuously improving performance. For these to be effective they must also be in line with the aims, objectives and principal activities of the organization.

In short, the long-term success or failure of any organization depends upon the quality of its workforce in general and its management in particular. They must possess relevant skills both individually and collectively in order to provide the organization with its most central source of added value and competitive advantage.

Profit as a measure of performance

In focusing on profit it is not intended to apply a particular value to it in terms of its superiority to other objectives an organization will invariably have. Indeed, most (if not all) organizations are measured on a much wider range of factors than just their financial position. However, what is being acknowledged is that profit, as measured by return on capital, is, in the long run, the ultimate measure of an organization's performance and skills in terms of the use it makes of the resources and assets at its disposal. Because of this, it is an excellent starting point for analysis.

Nor is it being suggested that profit maximization is necessarily the name of the game—indeed, the level of profits to be sought is essentially a management decision. However, it does need to be recognized that for most (if not all) organizations, profits or, in the case of not-for-profit organizations, surplus revenues after expenses are a cost of staying in business. Moreover, given the financial system in which organizations operate, it is generally important that they generate real returns in order to justify the investment by their owners and provide for future development.

One further point to note here relates to the *quality* of profits. Many trainers are unfamiliar with this notion, and its inference that some profits are better than others. Well, in terms of reflecting the capacity of an organization to survive, some are! Think, for a moment, about your own organization. To what extent are its profits, or surpluses, dependent upon, for example, products and services where added value is minimal? Are they cyclical? Are they dependent upon reducing inventories or customers whose ability to pay is doubtful?

From a different angle, to what extent are profits the result of financial manipulation, and so on? To the extent that they are, it could be argued that they are inferior to those generated from mainstream business activity and sound practices. Where this is the case it is almost certain that the skills of the workforce in adding value need to be developed.

Perhaps the issue of the quality of earnings should be taken further. For example, some would argue that the use of return on capital as the key indicator of performance is not relevant to particular industries or sectors or can give dangerously misleading signals. (For a more detailed discussion of this see Sveiby and Lloyd, 1987.) Their real concern is that insufficient account is taken of 'knowhow' capital as a result of the pressure to focus on the development of financial capital in order to satisfy the interests of their shareholders.

Of course, such dangers are inherent in focusing on the measurement of performance in financial terms, just as there are in any system of measurement—whatever system is in use, it is always important to 'check the figures'. If this check shows, for example, that high returns on capital are being earned at the expense of investment in people and knowhow capital, then management is almost certainly failing to recognize the long-term needs of the business.

Public sector and not-for-profit organizations

Many readers of this book are likely to be concerned with or work in public sector or in not-for-profit organizations, such as charities. They may, therefore, be wondering how the model applies to them. This is not a question that can be answered easily because of the diversity of types of organization which these sectors comprise.

On the one hand, there are nationalized industries. These do have outputs which are readily measured in financial terms and already apply a wide range of financial disciplines and management accounting techniques. Where they are different from private sector businesses is the balance between their financial and non-financial objectives. In many countries a number of these industries have been (or are) in the process of being returned or transferred to the private sector. However, even when this has been completed, the problem of deciding the rate of return to be achieved as a basis for measuring performance still remains.

On the other hand, there are services which are seen as being central to the public sector and whose objectives are framed in very broad terms. A good example of this is local government and the very wide range of responsibilities they hold, ranging from refuse collection to education. In these organizations, financial performance tends to have traditionally focused on the control of inputs and their costs. In consequence, their financial disciplines and reporting systems have been shaped by the priority given to budget preparation and control in order to operate within revenue constraints.

Yet even here things are changing. A simple (though perhaps unsatisfactory) example is the subcontracting of ground maintenance, cleaning and school meals. Much more fundamental is the introduction of schemes of devolved financial management. Although the suggestion that schools are being transformed from cost to profit centres might seem to be going too far, it is interesting to reflect that they are in competition with independent schools, some of which have clearly formulated profit objectives.

The development of such schemes shifts the focus of the organization and requires a better balance between the management of inputs and outputs. In the process, they provide a framework in which managers, the heads and governors of schools must set clear objectives for their own establishments. They are also given considerable freedom to make decisions on how best to allocate resources and respond to changes in local conditions and needs. These changes create their own special needs for heads, and others, to acquire skills in general and financial management.

Finally, Training for Profit is not intended to be a universally appropriate system, but a systematic approach. As such, it offers a framework which can be adapted to different objectives and settings. The concepts and disciplines which underpin it therefore have much to offer public sector and not-for-profit organizations in their search to find ways of providing better value for money.

The importance of added value

For trainers, understanding the link between added value, training and profit is crucial. Its importance is reflected in the basic model of the 'Training for Profit cycle' (Figure 2.1). This shows how, from the starting point of capital, resources in the form of operating assets are transformed by the workforce into products and services. In the process, added value is realized from sales and revenues, resulting in profits.

Essentially, added value can be considered as the income generated through sales in excess of material costs. Increases in sales which are merely eaten up by increases in material costs do not result in greater added value. Unless they form part of a wider strategy—for example, to

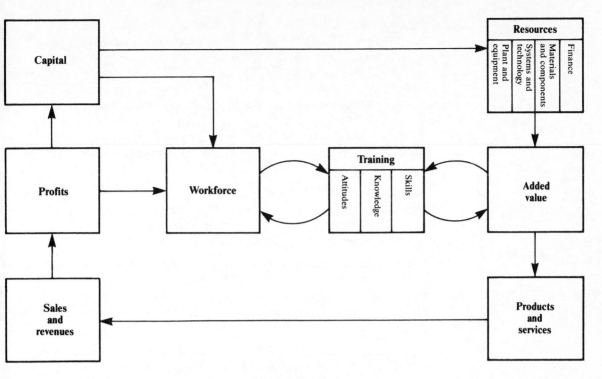

Figure 2.1 *The Training for Profit cycle*

secure wider distribution or some other form of competitive advantage—such increases are likely to be futile.

Many factors influence the added value of a business—its history, objectives and strategies, basic resources and economic context. However, the prime determinant of a firm's added value is its skills in managing:

1 Inputs—for example, buying, storing and controlling materials
2 Processes—i.e. transforming inputs into products and services
3 Outputs—for example, the marketing, sales and distribution of its products and services

The organization's workforce is central to all of these factors and activities, and the extent to which total revenues generated exceed the basic input costs of materials—i.e. added value—must also reflect the level of appropriate skills they possess.

Elements of the approach

However, skills are not the whole story. The Training for Profit approach involves taking a broad view of the organization, including its business objectives, methods of operating and basic resources in addition to the quality and effectiveness of its staff. It also takes into account the organization's past, present and future as well as the environment in which it operates.

This means that the trainer has to consider two overall perspectives: one describing how the business appears to be, the other reflecting what it needs to look like at some point in the future. It is the difference between these two images which serves as the source for identifying the underlying strengths and weaknesses of the whole organization and for planning how to fill the gap between current performance and plans for the future. Forming such perspectives is a complex process and it is unlikely that the quantity and complexity of the information involved can be handled without the application of conceptual frameworks and analytical tools.

Beyond an awareness of the organization's fundamental objectives and performance, the trainer also needs to understand the significance of the underlying organizational processes. It is these which really determine the effectiveness of the transformations of inputs into outputs.

In particular, the trainer needs to be aware of the processes relating to strategy, structure and culture. Without such an awareness it will not be possible to understand the organization's performance. Nor will it be possible to pinpoint and assess accurately the underlying training implications, needs and opportunities.

For example, changes in strategy inevitably call for changes in attitude, knowledge and skills. Trainers therefore need to be able to identify these changes and assess the training needed to bring them about.

In terms of an organization's structure it is important to identify not just its effectiveness but also the knowledge and skills required to work effectively within it. Only by doing so and providing appropriate training will it be possible to ensure that it is responsive to the demands put upon it. More than this, structure is a determinant of career paths and opportunities. It is therefore fundamental to balancing the needs of the organization with those of the individual.

The same can be said of culture, though this is even more important in determining levels of productivity and individual satisfaction than structure. Yet how many organizations provide adequate training to enable their employees to work effectively within it?

Trainers also need to appreciate that for an organization to achieve its objectives it must relate effectively to its environment. For example, in times of recession the skills of controlling costs and maintaining existing customers are paramount. More than this, at any point of the economic cycle, management needs to possess the skills to integrate the very different activities inside and outside the organization. In effect, it is in a constant state of flux and has to adapt, for example, to:

- The level of economic activity
- The degree of industrial efficiency and competitiveness
- The level and stage of development of technology
- The level of socio-political stability

- The quality and quantity of human resources and the associated aspects of the education and training system
- Government policy on intervention
- Government responsiveness to economic developments
- The availability of natural resources
- International trends and developments

Towards a synthesis

In any business, an important function of management is to be skilled in differentiating the elements that contribute to the organization's success in providing products and services, and then integrating them to form an effective organization. This role is central to its ability to generate profits, be adaptive and thus survive (Elliott, 1989).

The elements which require differentiation and integration are reflected in Figure 2.2, the basic Training for Profit model. All of these are, of course, interrelated and hence result in the need for general managers in particular, and others to varying degrees, to possess appropriate skills in understanding and using them to ensure profitability and survival.

The Training for Profit approach therefore calls on the trainer to possess a particular awareness of the organization's business objectives, competitive strategy and performance. It is only by being aware of all these aspects of the business that training investment can be balanced between the development of long-term organizational effectiveness and the achievement of satisfactory performance in the short term.

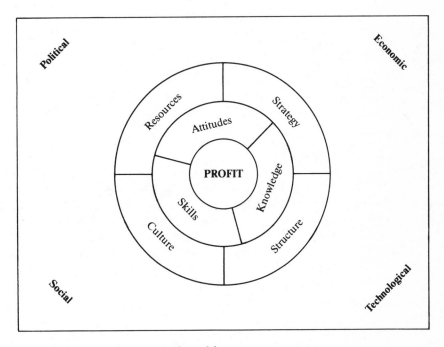

Figure 2.2 *The Training for Profit model*

Application of the approach

At this level, the approach demands the application of conceptual and perceptual skill in order to form an overview of the business. It is only through the accurate perception of business practicalities that the various strategic training questions can be addressed.

By using the Training for Profit approach, those with specific responsibility for training can consider the following kinds of issues:

- What is the general nature and rate of change in the various elements of the environment? What is their likely impact on the organization and what are the implications for the workforce in terms of attitudes, knowledge and skills?
- Which specific developments in the environment does the organization need to take account of (for example, labour market trends, competitive activity, legislation, distribution patterns, information technology)?
- What is the overall level of profitability of the firm? Does it imply priority needs for improvement (for example, through immediate cost reduction) or maintenance and development through control of costs and increasing revenue-generating activities? To what extent are the attitudes, knowledge and skills of the workforce consistent with these priorities?
- What is the source of the organization's revenues and profits? How stable are these and how will gaps be filled? What does this imply for the organization's mix of skills?
- Within the organization's cost structure, which elements are most in need of control? What is the provision of training to ensure this?
- What is the degree of consistency between the organization's resources, strategy, structure and culture? Where are there shortcomings and conflicts between the components and what sort of training might be appropriate to remedy them?
- How well integrated is the organization with its environment? Where are the mismatches and what are the training implications?
- What are the organization's major strengths and weaknesses in terms of skills? How does the overall mix of these skills impact upon profitability and organizational effectiveness?
- Given the context of the organization in its environment, what general and particular management skills are required? How can the appropriate balance between breadth and depth be developed?
- What are the implications, opportunities and constraints for the development of career structures? What mix of formal training and planned experience should be provided?
- How effective is the organization's training system in identifying and meeting needs? How does it, and the training provided, compare with competitors' systems?

Assessing performance and potential

It can be seen that, in applying the Training for Profit approach, the trainer is examining the organization as a whole, even though the main training needs and opportunities may lie in one functional area. It is therefore important to work from the general to the particular, from overall strategy and measures of performance to the reasons for unsatisfactory performance. Within these contexts, specific parts of the organization can then be examined in detail.

Consistent with the need for the trainer to possess an awareness of the strategy and performance of the organization, an appreciation of business finance is also vital. At one level, this is because organizations have objectives expressed in financial terms. At another, it is because the financial structure and results of the organization can be used to reflect the allocation of resources, its performance, strengths, weaknesses and potential. They can also be used for assessing almost every part and function of it.

The trainer can thus reach an understanding of what training may be needed in order to contribute to the improvement and development of the organization's performance and effectiveness. It also provides the professional, sharp and credible base from which to argue the case for training investment, training design and implementation.

Financial analysis

Central to this approach of understanding the organization is the analysis of financial statements and the application of the techniques of financial ratio analysis. These techniques provide the tools for measuring changes in the financial structure and results of a business. They also reflect the decision-making skills of management in allocating resources and those of the entire workforce in making the best use of them. Consequently, financial analysis serves as the basis for assessing and reflecting the performance of the organization and the underlying needs and opportunities for training to contribute to its performance and effectiveness in both the short and longer terms.

A review of financial statements is given in Appendix 1 and an explanation of the techniques of financial ratio analysis is provided in Chapters 6 and 7, but their potential in the overall assessment of training needs is given here. Their significance should not be missed, for they enable the trainer to begin to consider the following key questions:

- What is the overall financial picture indicated by the figures for the current year? For example,
  Is there sufficient liquidity, profit and capital?
  How strong or weak is the business in financial terms?
  Has it borrowing potential?
  To what extent is it taking too much credit or failing to control debtors or stock levels?
  What is the gap between current performance and that planned for the future?

- What is the picture reflected in the trends over a period of years. For example:
  What is happening to levels of profitability?
  Is the business growing or contracting?
  Is productivity rising or falling?
  Is liquidity and solvency increasing or decreasing?

Training focus

The trainer can then go on to ask further questions about the implications of the information revealed. For example:

- What questions does this raise about the company's policies, procedures and methods of operating? Does management appear to be in control of the business? To what extent might issues of decision making, organization and job design be involved?
- Where do the major strengths and weaknesses, problems and opportunities appear to lie? What would seem to be areas for priority action? What sort of benefits might be expected to result from tackling them? What would be the likely impact on profitability?
- What does it suggest about the general level of skills in managing the business and those in operating its component parts and major functions? Does it suggest that management is well informed and acts upon the information available to them?
- What are the possible implications and priorities for exploiting areas where skills exist and remedying deficiencies?

In assessing and forming an overview of the training needs of an organization it is clearly important to ensure a balance between short- and longer-term needs. It can therefore be instructive to consider in which areas it traditionally tends to focus its training priorities and investment, even though they are essentially interrelated.

Does it, for example, give priority to building assets or responsiveness in order to survive, or does it concentrate on developing a learning and problem-solving orientation which enables it constantly to adapt to its environment? In turn, to what extent is this consistent with the needs and opportunities facing the business?

It will often be found, for example, that training budgets are primarily allocated to developing tangible resources and systems and procedures rather than developing the less-visible alternatives in the areas of strategy, structure and culture. The consequence of this can be the attainment of little more than marginal improvements in efficiency, particularly where the organization is already asset-rich and 'physically' rather than 'cerebrally' strong. Conversely, investing training resources 'below the line' in the processes of developing its competitive strategy—and hence key operating policies—can result in dramatic improvements in effectiveness.

The organization 'in trouble'

These considerations can be particularly pertinent to understanding an organization which appears to be 'in trouble'. They support the analysis that organizations rarely get into difficulties suddenly, but embark on a process over a considerable period of time—generally years (Argenti, 1976; Davis, 1988). However, signs of difficulty may be hard to recognize because the pressures on members of the organization, particularly managers, to conceal the reality not just from the outside world but also from themselves can be very strong. In such organizations it will often be observed that their objectives lack consistency and validity. This can be seen to be a product of attitudes and values of those in positions of authority which manifest themselves in the organization's structure and culture. Consequently, too much reliance is placed on the skills of particular individuals at the expense of teamwork. This results in a lack of breadth and depth of management skills across the organization. In turn, the development and contribution of employees is inhibited and restricted.

On closer examination, these organizations will also often be found to have insufficient skills and defective systems, particularly in the crucial areas of budgeting, costing and financial control. The result of this situation is likely to be that the organization lacks the capacity to respond to change and this manifests itself in the progressive deterioration of its resources, i.e. products and services, plant, marketing skills and employee relations. Not surprisingly, its underlying financial position also deteriorates.

Where such symptoms are apparent it is not only the attitude, knowledge and skill requirements implied by the organization's objectives and competitive strategy which need investigation but also the process by which they are formulated and determined. If this is not done, the organization is likely to continue down the path to failure.

The importance of process

Figure 2.3 shows the Training for Profit approach in terms of process, from the starting point of the review of the organization's strategy through to the validation and evaluation of training investment. Carrying out this comprehensive form of examination of the organization ensures that key areas where training can contribute to improved performance and better use of underused assets are identified.

However, it is the actual process of carrying out the assessment of the strengths and weaknesses of the organization and their translation into skills that is the key to success. It is by implementing this process that the trainer really has the opportunity to reflect where, why, how and when training can help to improve and develop the performance and effectiveness of the organization in both the short and long terms.

It is, for example, through process that the trainer obtains agreement and commitment to the analysis of the major training priorities within the organization as well as an understanding of potential training contri-

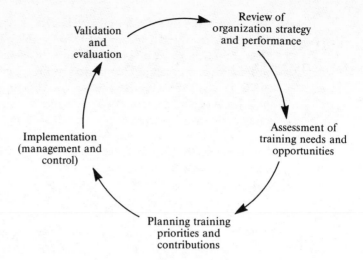

Figure 2.3   Training for Profit as a process

Figure 2.4   Training for Profit's virtuous circle

butions to improved performance in measurable terms—i.e. profits. Further, since the process involves looking to the future to identify the training required to achieve performance objectives, it serves as an integrating device, supporting and encouraging the planning activities of managers. This is not only beneficial to the organization at every level, it is also central to the promotion of the more effective use of the workforce.

This process of integrating training investment and activity with organizational objectives and performance is fundamental in creating understanding of the training contribution. Properly executed, it is highly pervasive and a very powerful source of energy and stimulus leading to what is essentially a virtuous, circular process shown in Figure 2.4.

Further still, it is only by possessing and applying such knowledge and skills that trainers can really help those with responsibility for implementing training—whether chief executives, directors, functional heads or line managers—to diagnose their situation and assess where training can contribute to the business. How else can the essential training contribution really be assessed? How else can appropriate and effective training strategies and plans really be developed? And how else can appropriate levels of training investment really be determined?

The training contribution

There is no more important challenge facing managers than that of ensuring that their organizations possess the appropriate attitudes, knowledge and skills to improve, continuously, overall effectiveness. This requires both managers and trainers to have the ability to assess the skill and training needs and opportunities which will generate real returns for their organizations and be able to translate them into priorities and plans. Paradoxically, it might also be said that, in many ways, the Achilles' heel of the trainer lies in the difficulty experienced in demonstrating the value of the training contribution in the terms most valued by managers—i.e. money. Within these contexts the Training for Profit approach provides not only a means for assessing and planning training needs but also a way to stimulate awareness, interest and investment in training.

References

Argenti, J. (1976) *Corporate Collapse: the causes and symptoms*, New York: McGraw-Hill.

Davis, D. (1988) *How to Turn a Company Round: a practical guide to company rescue*, Cambridge, Director Books.

Elliott, J. (1989) *Training Needs and Corporate Strategy*, IMS Report No. 164, Institute of Manpower Studies.

Sveiby, K.E. and T. Lloyd (1987) *Managing Knowhow*, London: Bloomsbury.

Conclusion to Part One

There is no more important challenge facing managers than that of ensuring that their organizations possess the appropriate skills to improve, continuously, overall effectiveness. The reason for this is that skills are the basic and central source of an organization's effectiveness. Thus, whatever its objectives, every organization needs to decide how best to allocate its resources and skills in order to optimize its productive capacity. In the process it needs to develop its training systems and capacity for learning in order to ensure understanding and the ability to cope with the variety and nature of challenges facing it. Only by doing so will it be possible to balance and integrate the needs of the organization and its members with the demands of the environment.

This reflects the role and importance of training in bringing together and underpinning all the activities of the organization. It also provides the essential starting point for creating a workforce with the attitudes, knowledge and skills to develop the business. To achieve this, trainers need to be able to carry out a proper assessment of training needs. Training for Profit serves as a means for doing so. It provides a systematic approach and offers a framework which can be adapted to different objectives and settings.

In the process, it ensures that key areas where training can contribute to improved performance and better use of underused assets are identified. It also provides the professional, sharp and credible base from which to argue the case for training investment, training design and implementation.

As a starting point for reviewing your organization's approach to training, here are some questions you might like to consider:

To what extent:

- Do senior management recognize and accept their overall responsibility for training?
- Are line managers able to formulate clear expectations of the role of training and its contribution and to fulfil their own direct responsibility for it?
- Are business plans available as a basis for assessing training needs?
- Is training investment directed towards, and integrated with, the needs of the business?

- Do trainers have the capacity to contribute fully to the development of the organization and its workforce at a strategic level?

As a process:

- How are training needs assessed?
- What are the strengths and weaknesses of the assessment process?
- How might it be improved?
- What are the obstacles in doing so?
- How might they be overcome?

PART TWO

Strategy, structure and culture

Introduction The overall assessment of training needs involves taking a broad view of the organization, its objectives, methods of operating, basic resources and the quality and effectiveness of its workforce. In the process, account needs to be taken of its past, present and future and its environmental context. This implies the need for the trainer to produce a range of overall perspectives—for example, in terms of how the business appears to be and what it needs to look like at some future point in time. In turn, it is the difference between these images which serves as the source for identifying the underlying strengths and weaknesses of the organization in terms of skills and the consequential analysis of training opportunities and needs. In the process, it will ensure that the training plans subsequently developed are consistent with the overall needs of the organization.

Forming such perspectives is a complex process, and it is unlikely that the quantity and complexity of information can be handled without the application of conceptual frameworks and tools of analysis in order to create order and provide for logical analysis. For, what is ultimately required, is a synthesis of all the components of the organization and their respective contributions to added value.

In order to identify its overall training needs the trainer must be able to form an overview of:

- an understanding of the organization's implicit, as well as explicit, strategy, including a broad awareness of the interests of its stakeholders
- the organizational processes by which strategy is determined and implemented, especially those relating to structure and culture

Only by possessing an awareness of all these factors can the implications for skills and training really be assessed. Without it, it will not be possible to identify, let alone ensure, the appropriate attitudes, knowledge and skills that management and the workforce need to possess consistent with the goals and tasks to be achieved. In practice, of course, these elements are inextricably linked. However, for the trainer seeking to understand the business it is helpful to consider them as separate interlocking components.

It is worth noting that there is an implicit assumption here, i.e. that success is attributable to the skills of sound management and an appropriately trained workforce. However, I can't imagine that many trainers have difficulty with this notion, though providing evidence to support it is more difficult. Indeed, where evidence has been obtained (for example, those companies in Peters' and Waterman's book *In Search of Excellence*) success has generally been shown to be no more than an elusive and ephemeral phenomenon—some would even say, random event.

To counter this, I like to think of the apocryphal story attributed to Gary Player, the South African golfer, on winning a major US tournament. Having holed on the 18th a commentator is reported to have thrust a microphone into his face with the words 'Gee, Gary, you sure were lucky on the greens today, weren't you?' Measuring his reply carefully, Player is reported to have said 'Let me tell you something funny that I've discovered. I've found that the more I practise my putting, the luckier I get.'

The purpose of this part of the book is to present a basic analytical framework under the separate headings of strategy, structure and culture. The aim is to provide a set of tools which can be readily understood and which provide a starting point for the trainer to get a 'feel' for the business and identify potential training issues and needs. At a practical level, Appendix 2 includes an *aide-mémoire*, designed to assist in the process of reviewing an organization as a whole in order to understand its behaviour and performance and identify key areas where training can contribute to improved results.

3 Strategy

Its importance for trainers

The importance of strategy for trainers was brought home to me some years ago in my dealings with the chief executive of a large brewery. My task was to review the extent to which training being carried out in the company related to the needs of the business. After preliminaries about the general state of the trade, I asked the chief executive what he considered to be the company's main objective. 'To make a profit, of course,' he replied, somewhat testily and dismissively.

Though common enough, it struck me as an odd response, particularly in the context of what I understood to be the company's far from satisfactory trading position. Taking a deep breath, I decided to test him further by floating the question: 'How much profit are you looking for?'

The silence which followed was interesting, to say the least, as was the change in his complexion! It was evident that the business had neither a defined profit objective nor a considered strategy for making one. For him, and the business, profit would be no more or less than what might be left at the end of the day.

For me, the real lesson of this experience was the realization that, in many organizations, there is a huge shortfall in the skills of business planning. As a result, the overall issue of organizational strategy and the extent of success or failure in meeting the various objectives and interests of different stakeholders in a business is largely avoided, in the short run at least. However, from a training perspective, confronting these issues provides a unique opportunity to review the skills possessed and needed by the entire workforce and, especially, top management.

This experience also taught me that many people who mouth the objective of profit are paying no more than lip service to the concept of profit and have little understanding of its real significance as, for example, a cost of staying in business. By the same token, those who talk of the importance of 'the bottom line' or of human resources as their 'most precious assets' often seem engaged in no more than a form of rhetoric.

Although this example is drawn from some years ago, the problem of skill deficiencies in business planning remains very widespread today. An indication of the extent of this was provided in Chapter 1. It is also reinforced by recent findings that fewer than 25 per cent of company directors hold degrees or professional qualifications and only 8 per cent have received specific training for their role.[1] It is hardly surprising, therefore, to find that the majority of firms do not have formal business plans.

That said, many trainers would regard this sort of intervention as akin to treading on 'hallowed ground' and, to be fair, in some organizations the trainer who did so would need to be a brave soul. At the same time, trainers must recognize and accept that it is no more than a logical and emergent progression of the trainer's role and contribution.

Developing understanding

Trainers seeking to develop their understanding of strategy can do no better than to consider the work of Michael Porter (1980, 1985), one of Harvard's most successful business gurus. His starting point is that the state of competition in an industry depends on five basic competitive forces, namely:

1 The threat of new entrants to the industry
2 The intensity of rivalry among existing firms
3 The threat of substitute products or services
4 The bargaining power of buyers
5 The bargaining power of suppliers (Porter, 1985).

It is the collective strength of these forces that determines the ultimate profit potential. For the trainer, the value of the knowledge of these underlying sources of competitive pressure is implicit in Porter's statement that it

highlights the critical strengths and weaknesses of the company, animates its positioning in its industry, clarifies the areas where strategic changes may yield the greatest payoff, and highlights the areas where industry trends promise to hold the greatest significance as either opportunities or threats (1980, p.5).

Once specified, therefore, the concept of strategy can be used to guide the overall behaviour of the firm—hence its significance for the trainer in assessing training needs.

Of particular value is Porter's research into what he terms generic strategies. His starting point is his finding that, in order to achieve competitive advantage, organizations face a basic choice of competing in terms of either cost or differentiation, i.e. achieving a price premium by adding value in the form of superior products, service and delivery. Within these options management then has to decide whether to pursue a broad- or narrow-based approach to the market (for example, through seeking overall leadership or niche orientation).

Porter argues that it is the emphasis of focus on a particular generic strategy that distinguishes successful from unsuccessful organizations. For him, the biggest error is to get stuck in the middle. One does not have to agree with his analysis. For example, Lord Weinstock, Chief Executive of GEC, once described a niche as a potential tomb, and Tom Peters (1989) maintains that a cost-based focus contains the seeds of its own destruction, being 'ultimately fragile and vulnerable to the clever differentiator, which will likely win both the customers and the profits over the medium to long term" (p.62).

Despite these caveats, as a model it provides a useful way of 'positioning' an organization in the context of potential strategies and, according to its position, certain implications for training will be immediately apparent. By way of example, a business focusing on a low-cost orientation will need to ensure that the attitude of its workforce is consistent with this. In turn, it will need to develop particular skills in the provision and use of cost-based information. It may be that controlling costs will require a high degree of standardization and that, in turn, this implies excellence in a relatively narrow range of skills. The high degree of standardization and control may call for a greater amount of hierarchy in the organization structure than would otherwise be the case, impacting upon such factors as management style, career progression and the reward system, both material and psychological.

In contrast, the organization focused on differentiation is likely to need to develop attitudes which reflect the importance of the customer. This is not to suggest that costs will not be regarded as important and requiring careful control, but the degree of emphasis will be different. Similarly, to satisfy customer needs is likely to require a high degree of flexibility, not just in terms of the workforce but also relating to the organization's structure, its technology and information systems in use. Only through flexibility is it likely that customer requirements for superior product performance, service and delivery will be met. This, in turn, is likely to call for a workforce with breadth of skills and a high degree of individual accountability, combined with teamwork and a management structure to suit.

Getting started

Where to start? What is it, without attempting to become corporate planners or chief executives, that trainers need to know about business objectives, strategies and plans in order to make a qualitative judgement about the skills of those with responsibility in this domain and also so as to be able to contribute to discussion at this level and ensure the connection between business plans and skill and training needs?

Although in terms of intervention strategy there can be many points of entry, at a conceptual level it is helpful to start by considering the stakeholders in a business. The reason for this is that their interests provide the context in which, whether conscious or not, business policy and strategy are formed. This chapter therefore continues by looking at the various interest groups, followed by an examination of the elements of strategy and, finally, a discussion of the implications for training.

Stakeholder interests

Although all the parties to a business may have an interest in its success, the extent to which interests can be separate and different is often overlooked. Such differences come into stark contrast when, for example, in times of difficulty, the directors have to decide the balance of misery to be endured by shareholders—for example, in the form of lesser or even passed dividends, or financial restructuring, possibly diluting shareholder interest—and employees in the form of wage restraint, or even wage cuts, loss of jobs and job security. Such choices also, of course, have to be made when times are 'good', though in these circumstances there is likely to be a much higher degree of integration between the interests of the different parties since there is an enlarged cake to share.

Although the particular interests of different groupings will differ from one organization to another and according to such factors as its history, ownership, size and activities, a useful framework is provided by an overall consideration of shareholders, top management, employees and the community or economy in which it operates.

Shareholders

Although there may be differences of interest between different groups of shareholders (for example, financial institutions, directors and employees) in the sense that the shareholders' relationship to the company is generally separate from its management activity, it is primarily a financial one concerned with investment and returns thereupon. Such stakeholders are therefore likely to be interested in:

- The rate of return relative to the market and risks involved
- Increasing value of the investment—for example, as reflected in the share price, earnings per share and market capitalization
- Maintenance and growth of dividends
- Increased utilization of assets of the business as measured by returns on shareholders' capital

Top management

The on-going debate on both sides of the Atlantic over 'top people's' pay and the role of non-executive directors provide examples of the potential for conflicts of interests between the different stakeholders. Thus, while top management may share the interest of shareholders in the efficient use of assets, particularly where focus may be sharpened by their rewards (for example, in the form of profit-related pay and share options) or by shareholder pressure groups, they are also likely to have a quite separate interest. In essence, this interest can often be seen to be related to the growth of the business in terms of its size rather than its efficiency.

This is not to say that directors and senior management are not interested in profits. Indeed, they have a strong interest in at least the stability of profits as a basis for personal security. However, for many, it is generally size rather than efficiency which really determines the degree of power, responsibility and rewards and career opportunities open to them within the organization.

Being cynical for a moment, readers long in the tooth may recall the coining of the term 'the nursing school of management', illustrating that one way to get ahead was to identify a problem and nurture it carefully until it was of a size to warrant senior management attention—for which, of course, the incumbent was the natural choice! Underlying the issue of size, however, is the inference that for many, the management of growth provides a high degree of satisfaction and is therefore intrinsically motivating.

Thus, unless deliberately aligned with shareholders' interests, top management's minds are likely to be on:

• Increasing sales income
• Expanding capital employed
• Maintenance of profitability
• Increasing cash flow

Cash flow is particularly important to this group since it reflects the degree of freedom they possess to make and realize their plans. It can be either positive (i.e. a net inflow) or negative (a net outflow). However, it is important to distinguish between cash which is generated internally as opposed to externally (for example, by raising capital in the form of shares or loans).

It can perhaps readily be understood that whereas positive internally generated cash flow leaves directors relatively free to chart and determine their own courses of action, recourse to external funds may render them subject to considerable scrutiny. As those who follow the financial press will have observed, such scrutiny can cause even the chairmen and senior officers of major companies to lose their jobs and yet others to seek to escape from public ownership.

Employees

Many directors feel uncomfortable with the notion that employees' interests, especially those of middle managers, might be separate from their own, for they often hold and have a vested interest in promoting a 'unitary' frame of reference. Thus it is natural that they should promote the notion that 'what is good for the company is good for employees'. However, in a general sense, the reality is perhaps reflected better in the extent to which society can be seen to contain many class divisions, both social and material, and, for example, in terms of inequality of opportunity in education, training and careers.

More specifically, many people's predominant experience of work and employee relations has been in the context of bureaucratic organizational structures, and the rigidity, rules and procedures which underlie them. They have therefore been socialized to want security and stability of employment at a time when, with major industrial restructuring under way, many are having to face up to the reality of reduced career opportunities and increased prospects of redundancy, job losses and high levels of unemployment. Thus the interests of those working in organizations can be seen, in the short term at least, to be in stark contrast to those making the decisions and to lie in:

- Increases in numbers employed
- Increasing labour component in sales
- Increases in the average rate of staff costs, including training
- Increases in the share of added value

The extent to which middle managers should be regarded as sharing the interests of employees or top management is likely to be a function of a whole range of factors, including, for example, the size of the organization, its financial performance, the basis of their reward, both material and psychological, and the extent of bureaucracy and unionization.

Community/ economy

Many organizations have historically reflected a high degree of concern for the community in which they operate. Such concerns range, for example, from willingness to comply with legislation and pay (rather than avoid) taxes to making provisions for health and safety, ecological and environmental protection, taking initiatives for the young and unemployed and providing sponsorship of the arts. However, it is only relatively recently that, with increased general public awareness and the emergence of powerful pressure groups, that organizations, especially large ones, have more or less been compelled to demonstrate their public responsibility and accountability. For the most part, these issues can be seen to be indicative of and subordinate to the community interest in wealth creation, both quantitative and qualitative. Expressed in specific financial terms, the community's interests in an organization can generally be equated with:

- Increases in turnover of capital
- Increases in profits and profitability
- Increased capital/expenditure on assets
- Increases in overseas earnings

The community has an interest in increases in the rate of turnover of capital by an organization (i.e. sales per unit of capital) in that it reflects efficiency in the use of a scarce resource. Similarly, increased profits and profitability are desirable if they reflect effectiveness of its use and the health of the organization.

The measure of capital per employee is consistent with the notion that wealth creation and competitive advantage are derived from capital investment. Although the exhortation 'export or die' has been a siren call for many organizations, given the inexorable growth of world trade, a community needs overseas earnings not just to provide increased prosperity and consumer choice but also to enhance its competitive ability.

It can be seen that such measures do not really pay due regard to the wider interests of society. One could argue, also, that the community is interested in such factors as investment in training or product prices, quality, choice, and their recycling potential. However, on the basis that the overall context in which organizations operate and communities exist is predominantly based upon the principles of capitalism and free enterprise, they provide a useful starting point for analysis.

At the same time, it needs also to be recognized that there can be a high degree of coincidence between the interests of other stakeholders in an organization and the community in which it operates. Thus, for example, producers of motor vehicles have a vested interest in tackling the environmental problems of waste, traffic pollution and congestion. Failure to address them will not augur well for future sales! Further, such problems open up business opportunities (for example, for product recycling and development, traffic management and flow systems) in their own right and which such organizations may be extremely well placed to tackle.

While on this theme it should also be noted that just as Japanese industry has taught the world that 'quality' is cost effective and a tool of competitive strategy, the same can generally be said about environmental care. For example, production processes low in pollution are often highly efficient in terms of energy consumption and wastage. Thus a cost advantage can be achieved as well as a competitive one in selling environmentally attractive products.

Elements of strategy

Top management's attempts to balance the interests of the various stakeholders leads to the development of business strategy and the goals for profits and profitability. This applies even where there is no formal planning system—for although they may be informal, unwritten and even unconsciously derived, they are implicit in management's actions and behaviour. Inherent within them is the need to assess their implications for the skills of the workforce. Failure to do so not only jeopardizes the prospects of realizing the organization's goals, it also undermines its integration.

Essentially, business policies reduce to decisions about:

- Increasing sales volume
- Developing product mix
- Determining prices
- Controlling costs

This simple policy framework contains the basic elements for the determination of profits. Some would add a further element—reducing capital employed—though for the majority of businesses, unless they engage in off-balance-sheet activities or distribution of reserves to shareholders, it is, in practical terms, difficult and rare. Despite its simplicity, however, the mix of potential strategic options within it is infinite. They include, for example:

- *Acquisition and merger*, whether to pursue growth, improve cash flow or gain market entry or standing.

- *Joint ventures or alliances*, whereby organizations develop collaborative arrangements with suppliers, competitors or customers, both within and across national boundaries; and ranging from sharing the costs of research and development to agreements on marketing and distribution.
- *Financing*—for example, the substitution of one form of debt for another so as to reduce the cost of capital, or the adoption of balance sheet management techniques such as the sale and leaseback of properties in order to provide alternative sources of funds.
- *Exporting*, whether through agents or distributors, or establishing a direct presence.
- *Importing*, whether as an end in itself or an alternative to local production.
- *Restructuring*—for example, as a means to reposition an organization in terms of its products and markets, through organization redesign, disposals or acquisitions.
- *Diversification*, whether in terms of products and/or markets and whether related—i.e. searching for synergy—or unrelated, as represented by an accumulation or portfolio of diversified products or businesses.
- *Research and development*—for example, in order to produce innovation in products or resources.
- *Pricing*—for example, geared towards achieving distribution and market share or an improvement in operating margins.
- *Productivity*—for example, through automation, computerization and information technology, standardization, rationalization or restructuring.
- *Organic growth*, i.e. through the expansion of existing activities.
- *Human resource management*, i.e. the strategic use of people to achieve competitive advantage.

It is important to understand the infinite nature of the potential mix of these options. In making their decisions management shape not just the strategy of the organization but also its ensuing structure and culture. It also needs to be appreciated that no one single policy or mix of policies provides the 'one best way'. In other words, different policies can be used to achieve the same ends. Management has to decide upon the strategic mix and the degree of reliance on, for example, a single overriding strategy or broadly based mix. (For an interesting discussion of this, see Newbould and Luffman, 1978.)

Implications for training

At a conceptual level, analysis of the various stakeholder interests provides an indication of the sorts of skills required to maintain and develop an organization. More specifically and practically, it provides an insight into managerial decision making. This is so because management has to decide how to balance the various interests of the different stakeholders—it simply is not possible to meet them all. Thus management has to decide who will be given preference over whom, and what priority to allocate to particular interests.

The resulting decisions impact upon the strategy, structure and culture of the organization and, according to the balance struck, reflect the different attitudes, knowledge and skills of top management in terms of both what is to be done and how it is to be accomplished. It is also important to be aware that, over a period of time, these attributes become embodied in the organization and shape its entire profile. In consequence, the organization and the skills it possesses can be seen to be and have been shaped by management's response to the decisions it has made in seeking to meet the interests of the various stakeholders.

Strategic decisions, therefore, not only reflect the attitudes, knowledge and skills of managment but also determine the needs for skills and training throughout the organization. For example:

- A shift towards exporting is likely to require additional skills in all aspects of marketing, product design, warehousing and distribution, finance, legal and commercial procedures and documentation, languages, etc. and will involve staff at all levels of the organization.
- Acquisitions and mergers, particularly where related to existing businesses, call for special skills of integration, for example in terms of creating cooperative relationships, common systems and procedures, and better utilization of plant and other resources. By the same token, joint ventures are likely to call for particular skills in, for example, the development of project management and negotiation based upon participation, trust and sharing to achieve a mutually satisfactory sharing of costs and benefits.
- Whereas financing may primarily appear to be a question of ensuring particular skills among a small number of corporate staff, in practice the ramifications are likely to impact widely. This is because such a strategy is likely to be accompanied by a sharp focus on cash flow management throughout the organization, including, for example, purchasing and purchase ledgers, invoicing, revenue accounting and stock control functions.
- Pricing calls for particular skills in controlling costs and marketing to plan for and ensure its effectiveness as a strategic tool. It is also likely to require special training of the sales force in negotiating skills (for example, in relation to discounts) and of the whole workforce if, in pursuing a strategy of achieving higher prices, added value is to be built into the product (for example, in terms of quality, delivery and service).

Conclusion

From these examples it can be seen that understanding an organization's strategy is fundamental to the process of identifying training needs and opportunities and planning for their implementation. They also show its interconnection with structure and culture. The process is, however, a complex one and can lead to many questions being raised before answers emerge. At the very least, in order to ensure the proper level of training investment and the relevance and coherence of training plans, trainers need to start by asking:

- What are the implicit training needs and opportunities?
- How should they be identified and planned for?
- What are the priorities within them?
- To what extent do they relate to the goals and strategy of the organization?
- Are they consistent with organizational policies?
- Are they achievable?
- Are the resources available for meeting them?
- Are there measures for gauging their fulfilment?

Note

1 Research carried out for the National Health Service Directorate by Warwick Business School (reported in *Management News*, July 1991).

References

Newbould, G.D. and G.A. Luffman (1978) *Successful Business Policies*, Aldershot: Gower.

Peters, T.J. (1989) *Thriving on Chaos*, London: Pan, p.62.

Porter, M.E. (1980) *Competitive Strategy: Techniques for Analyzing Industries and Competitors*, New York: The Free Press, p.5.

Porter, M.E. (1985) *Competitive Advantage*, New York: The Free Press.

4 Structure

In order to understand an organization's performance, trainers need not just knowledge of its strategy, financial structure and results but also awareness of its structure and culture. Without such an awareness it will not be possible to understand the human processes which so often reflect the training needs and opportunities to achieve improvements in organization effectiveness. In practice, structure and culture are inextricably intertwined. However, from the trainer's perspective of trying to understand the organizational behaviour it is helpful to consider them as separate interlocking components.

By way of example, a recent experience of working with a computer manufacturer should make the point. Having asked to see an organization chart to get an initial feel for its structure and design, I was told that it did not have one, the business having adopted a structure based on 'open architecture'. The idea, it seemed, was that by dispensing with charts, rigidity could be avoided and communication between staff increased. 'How do people find their way around?' I enquired. 'Oh,' replied my colleague with what seemed a twinkle in his eye, 'that's a process that can take years.'

The decision to abolish the charts had, of course, been taken by those who already knew their way around, having been in the business for years and, as is so often the case, had 'forgotten' the learning they had undertaken to get to where they were. And, of course, for all the lack of manifest structure, it was still extant in both a formal and an informal sense. In fairness, it should also be pointed out that the decision to dispense with charts was tied up with the organization's strategy of trying to meet the very diverse range of needs of its customers and also to introduce an element of competitiveness and 'creative tension' in the process.

However, for those seeking to design and manage induction and introductory training programmes you can perhaps imagine the situation to be fraught with difficulty. For those having to learn the ropes it was a nightmare. And for those who knew and who had to explain to those who did not, it was tedious, time consuming and frustrating. But people did talk to each other!

Conversely, this story puts me in mind of the director of a medium-size engineering business, for whom organization charts appeared to be a *sine qua non*. One of the uses he put them to was as a way of conducting regular forays to review the various and diversified sections of his business. On this particular occasion my colleague Williams—note the use of surnames here—had sensed an 'inspection' to be about due and tidied his office, and especially his desk, in anticipation. However, reckoning that he had at least minutes, if not hours, to spare, he was spending a few of them in reflection, leaning back in his chair, hands clasped behind his head and feet on desk.

His silent contemplation was broken by the sound of the door opening and the director's booming voice 'What do you think you're doing, Williams?' 'Thinking, Sir' he replied with a degree of circumspection. There followed a brief pause before the director's resounding riposte: 'You're not paid to think, Williams, you're paid to do! Get on with it!'

As with the earlier example, it is relevant to make the connection between this business's structure and its strategy. However, in this case, its customer base was very clearly defined—in fact, by statute—and its activities subject to regular scrutiny by government auditors.

These anecdotes reflect a number of important points. At one level they illustrate the inextricable link between strategy, structure and culture, and environmental context. Even so, in terms of the particular structures that might or might not have best suited either of these organizations, they were, in practice, also determined by the values of those in charge.

This highlights the way in which structure is both a determinant and a consequence of culture. It is particularly apparent when one considers the different degrees of freedom accorded to employees and the way in which authority appeared to be exercised. Such values can never be absolute, but reflect personal and individual models or images of what an organization should look like.

At another level, these examples suggest the extent to which skills are required of individuals not just to fulfil their specific tasks related to their work but also the sorts of skills necessary to operate effectively within the organization. At the very least, for example, working in an unstructured environment is likely to call for a depth of interpersonal skills, networking and building relationships that is very different from those of operating within a more rigidly defined framework.

Structure as a tool for assessing training needs

In practical terms, examining an organization's structure can be particularly helpful to trainers in understanding the needs for training associated with:

- The size of the organization and its complexity
- The location of particular individuals and their performance and contribution
- The division of work between individuals, departments and divisions, etc.
- Managers and subordinates, including the line and span of reporting responsibility

- The type of work being undertaken (for example, through job titles)
- The basis upon which activities are divided (for example, by function, product, market, geography, project, etc.)
- The degree of specialization
- The levels of management and hierarchy
- The means of coordination
- Possible areas of overlap and conflict
- Opportunities for continuous development and secondments
- Potential career paths
- A snapshot of workforce stability and possible succession needs (for example, by taking into account data such as age and length of service)
- Drawing inferences about the organization's behaviour and all that this implies for productivity, effectiveness and the provision of satisfying roles

The significance of size and form

Whatever the structure of an organization, staff need training in order to understand how it works and to gain their commitment to it. This is quite distinct from any functional or operational training that needs to be provided. More than this, studying an organization's structure can provide a very helpful basis for planning training interventions and assessing a wide range of training needs. However, to conduct this sort of analysis trainers need to be aware of the ways in which the structure of an organization and changes to it tend to impact upon the roles of its members and the relationships between them.

Idiosyncratic and functional structures

Small organizations, particularly those in the early stage of development, often provide only limited training and emphasis is placed on the recruitment of technically proficient staff. Such training as is provided will often be technically oriented to enable employees to develop their technical and specialist knowledge and skills. The bulk of training is likely to be in the form of learning on the job, and there is unlikely to be any recognizable system of planned development or career progression. Not surprisingly, as the organization grows, it often experiences pain as a result of its lack of skills and training in the non-technical functions of the business, such as finance, marketing and personnel.

As an organization develops it generally requires increased skills of coordination to manage and integrate its activities. Traditionally, such growth also tends to call for a more than proportionate increase in the number of managers required, particularly where a need is identified for it to be managed along more 'scientific' lines. In the process, priority for training investment is likely to be given to developing areas of functional competence. Additionally, an increasing level of interest is likely to be expressed in communications and 'managing' skills. It might also embrace an increasing interest in internal training to resolve issues of role clarification and the need to operate within, for example, budgetary systems and limits.

Shifting towards a functional structure can provide excellent opportunities for developing specialist skills and, through the concentration of numbers, professional development and career paths. At the same time, to achieve organizational effectiveness, such specialists will also need to be given an awareness of the 'world around them'. Without this, staff are unlikely to be sufficiently responsive to the needs of those around them, whether colleagues in other departments or customers.

Market structure

Increasing growth in size and competitive pressures often results in excessive strains being placed on a functional structure and leads an organization to move towards a product, market or geographic structure. This requires considerable training to shift the emphasis to the customer—to some extent mirrored in the increasing popularity and investment in customer-care programmes—and greater responsiveness to changing demands and situations. Failure to do so is likely to leave management's new 'mission statement'—often identifiable with this stage of organizational development—with a hollow ring and result in cynicism, sometimes amounting to despair, among employees.

To be effective, more specific training is likely to be required in product knowledge and customer service—not just for the sales force but throughout the whole organization, including, for example, switchboard operators, warehousing and delivery personnel, accounting clerks, purchasing staff, progress chasers, etc.

Albeit some years ago now, I shall always remember the example provided by the personnel manager of one of the major sherry houses. I had arrived early for our meeting and as a way, so to speak, of filling in my time, he invited me to sit through a couple of interviews he had scheduled so that I could see him 'at work'.

As the interviews progressed I remember thinking that the quality of the applicants he was seeing seemed to fall a long way short of what he had intimated he would be looking for. I was therefore left wondering why he seemed so concerned to grant such full and painstaking interviews, rather than getting shot of them as soon as decently possible! Later in the day, unable to contain my curiosity any longer, I put the question to him.

Without any sense of rebuke, though quite possibly deserved, he suggested that there was more than an evens chance that anyone he interviewed was also a consumer of his company's products. More than this, so were their friends. The last thing he wanted his department to do was to jeopardize sales by upsetting customers, whether existing or potential . . .

In presenting this example, it is worth drawing the distinction between the human value-driven approach which characterized this organization and those that are managed along far more 'scientific' principles. The latter are, in fact, even in the service sector, often far more bureaucratic than is commonly recognized (ask anyone who has worked for a major theme park or fast-food chain!).

In essence, the dividing point rests upon the extent to which management seeks to exercise its authority and exert central control over the workforce and its operations. The more it wishes to do so, the more will be the need to possess skills to develop and install formal systems and provide training to ensure the following of standarized and detailed procedures as the essential means of providing consistent standards and quality of products and service.

Such shifts also tend to be accompanied by increased devolution of financial accountability and the creation of additional profit and cost centres. Thus members require increased financial awareness in order to understand and fulfil their performance and contribution. This provides an example of how such structures call for individuals to be skilled in managing breadth as well as depth. It also reflects the pressure on staff to align their skills more closely to organizational rather than professional standards and fortunes. Such a change can be extremely threatening to the individuals involved and, to be successful, often requires a more open and supportive approach to personal development. Supervisors and managers are also likely to require additional skills in coordination and teamworking.

Finally, it is worth noting that, as the recent trends in restructuring being undertaken by many large companies indicate, developments in the use of information technology increasingly allow greater centralization of strategic and overall management functions, while also enabling the operating managerial function to be passed down the line—thus providing the scope for de-layering and a shift to flatter structures. To be successful, such measures and transformations imply the provision of training so that those involved are able to understand and fulfil their new and often wider responsibilities. Moreover, training is also essential to gaining commitment to the new structure, making the best use of information on operational performance and the IT system by which it is generated, and forming, developing and managing new working relationships.

Matrix structure

The degree of flexibility and collaboration inherently necessary in matrix organization requires employees to be highly adaptive and able to balance the often-competing demands implicit in task completion. It requires skills in project management, coordination, conflict resolution, teamworking and interpersonal relationships. Thus such organizations need to invest sensibly in human relations training. Underlying this is the need for the possession and development of maturity and attitudes at all levels—consistent with the goal of creating increased 'openness' in relationships within the organization and reduced levels of managerial control and authority. As can perhaps be imagined, in times when the 'going gets tough', those working within matrix structures are often unable to cope with the stress imposed upon them. The organization may, therefore, have to resort to the leaner, cleaner and meaner forms.

The problems associated with matrix management have given it something of a tarnished image. Even so, it is considerably more widespread than is often recognized, though not necessarily in its purest form. Indeed, in attempting to create the appropriate balance between depth and breadth and the coordination and integration of activities, most organizations can be seen to contain elements of a matrix structure. However, as noted earlier, the dividing line is the extent to which management relies on the enforcement of rules and procedures, as opposed to developing and trusting the capacity and potential of members of the workforce at all levels to handle increased responsibility.

Structural development

Given that the design of an organization needs to be consistent with its objectives, resources and environment, it must be able to adapt over time. The implication of this is that its design and structure at one stage of its development may not be suitable at another. The problem, therefore, from the trainer's point of view is to be able to identify the training needs associated with the alternative designs and structures and the various stages of transition.

A helpful model for considering these needs is provided by Larry E. Greiner (1976) and shown in Figure 4.1. It reflects the importance of pursuing effectiveness, rather than mere efficiency, by its focus on stages of organization growth and change. Greiner's central thesis is based on the idea that individual behaviour is determined primarily by previous events and experiences, rather than by what lies ahead. He therefore suggests that for many companies problems of organization and structure are rooted more in past decisions than in present events or outside market dynamics. As a result, he believes that managements often overlook such questions as:

- Where has our organization been?
- Where is it now?
- And what do the answers to these questions mean for where we are going?

In putting forward these ideas, Greiner was questioning the longstanding thesis, first proposed by Chandler (1962) in the USA, that outside market opportunities determine a company's strategy, which in turn determine the company's organization structure. In Greiner's view, organization structure is less malleable than Chandler assumed and, in fact, can play a critical role in influencing corporate strategy. Instead, organization development is, Greiner believes, based on five key elements:

1 Age of the organization
2 Size of the organization
3 Stages of evolution
4 Stages of revolution
5 Growth rate of the industry.

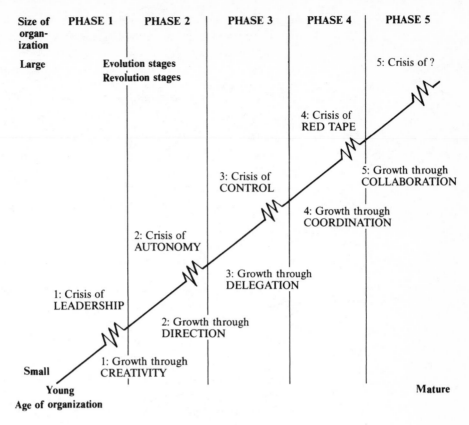

Figure 4.1   Greiner—the five phases of growth
Source: 'Evolution and Revolution as Organizations Grow', Larry E
Greiner, *Harvard Business Review on Management*, Heinemann, 1976.

The model is based on the analysis that, as an organization grows and
matures, it tends to pass through a series of phases. Each phase consists
of two stages: evolution and revolution. Evolutionary stages are characterized by prolonged periods of growth, during which there is little in
the way of major upheaval in organizational functioning. Revolutionary
stages, on the other hand, are periods of substantial turmoil in the
organization.

In considering the model it is important to understand its underlying
dynamic (and dialectic) nature. Thus each evolutionary stage causes its
own revolution. It also implies that each stage, both evolutionary and
revolutionary, is predictable.

The model was the forerunner of many derivatives and contributed significantly to those working in the area of organization development. But
what of its implications for trainers and the assessment of training
needs?

At an immediate level the trainer can use it to understand and reflect the likely training focus of the organization and the way that alternative forms of structure call for different sorts of skills and training provision. More fundamentally, it can be seen that, since the phases tend to be sequential, knowing where an organization is can help in the process not just of identifying immediate training needs but also in anticipating the needs likely to arise as the organization develops.

By way of example, each stage of evolution results not only in a different form of structure but also in changes in management focus and style. This, in turn, impacts upon the organization's control and reward systems. Knowing this should be helpful in planning and providing training to help in the process of transformation from one stage to another.

Thus, at one level, employees need training in the changed orientation, policies and practices of the organization. At another, they require general and specific training to equip them with knowledge and skills to fulfil their new or changed roles. Additionally, it can be seen that such developments have a significant impact on the career aspirations of employees and the career opportunities and structures within the organization. Thus, in looking at the organization and its development, specific plans can be made for employee development.

The model also highlights the need for considerable self-awareness on the part of top management, as well as the level of interpersonal skills needed in persuading other members of the organization of the need for change. In consequence, training can be designed and planned to mitigate the effects of an impending crisis and assist the organization's smooth transition.

Current examples of this can be seen in the public sector. Here, as with recent privatizations, there is an increasing shift from the traditional and longstanding bureaucratic structures to those based more closely on a market focus and performance targets determined not just by management but also by users and, in many cases, new shareholders. In the process, employees are likely to lose the safety of their traditional anonymity and will be required to take personal responsibility for their performance in the provision of services, whether they work in education, transport, health care, local authorities, or almost any other public sector organization.

These developments are likely to be accompanied by performance indicators and comparisons, including such measures as the quantity and quality of services provided, value for money, control of costs, resource utilization and return on investment. The extent and magnitude of these changes carry very important training implications, not just to enable members of these organizations to perform competently in their new roles and environment but also to facilitate the organization's transformation from one stage of development to another.

Organizational restructuring and development

Elsewhere the recent trend for commercial organizations to engage in substantial restructuring (including, for example, buy-outs, divestment, building core businesses, establishing joint ventures and alliances, and developing more flexible structures and strategies) illustrates the high incidence and increasing rate of organizational change. Fuelling this can be seen to be a number of factors, for example:

- The level of economic activity and point in the economic cycle
- The popularity of acquisitions within overall strategy and which often subsequently result in rationalization
- Secular change, particularly where industrial sectors are in decline
- Increasing international trade and the emergence of new markets and producers
- Technological change, especially relating to industrial processes and which result in a step-change, rendering existing methods and plants redundant
- Productivity pressures across all sectors, especially in the services sector, and particularly resulting from the more effective application of information technology
- Pressures to provide improved service and responsiveness to customers

Implications for training

Underlying these changes are the goals of improving competitiveness through the strengthening of market positions or developing new ones, on the one hand, and minimizing costs, on the other. Such changes are dependent upon the careful assessment of training needs and development of skills in the management of change. For example, at a general level, those affected are likely to require:

- An understanding of the goals of the organization and the business environment in which it is operating. Without this it will be hard to obtain support for change, particularly where it is seen as unnecessary or threatening
- A broader base of knowledge and skills to perform a wider range of job elements and cope with longer job cycles
- Increased flexibility and adaptability in order to work within a less hierarchical and more broadly based structure
- An ability to handle increased responsibility consistent with fewer layers of management
- A shift in management style and capacity to delegate
- An understanding of organizational processes and their impact upon efficiency and effectiveness

More specifically, it is likely that those involved will require:

- Additional knowledge and skills in order to fulfil wider responsibilities. This applies not just to the individual's traditional functional base, but also to the interfacing functions between which the boundaries are likely to become increasingly blurred and interdependent

- Enhanced skills in decision making and in the use of information and information technology, consistent with the individual's increased responsibility of operating within a flatter organization structure
- More developed communication, coordination and teamworking skills, consistent with increased levels of working across functions and boundaries
- A greater capacity for learning and coping with change, consistent with the increasing rate of change within a more flexible and responsive organization.

Thus, to be successful, comprehensive training of the workforce is required, right through from general awareness of the need for change to the specifics affecting the individuals involved and their jobs.

The danger is, however, that without proper training, the increasing pressures faced by operating management and employees will result in failure to achieve the strategic and operational goals of the organization and realize the potential benefits of restructuring. In addition there is likely to be the long-term and deep-seated cost of dissatisfied and resentful employees, underlined by an increasing sense of 'disenfranchisement' throughout the workforce.[1]

An important implication for organizations which stems from this is that much more attention needs to be given to the development of policies and skills for understanding and satisfying the psychological needs of their members. It also highlights the importance of developing shared objectives, a consistent identity, integrated employment policies and opportunities for personal development. In consequence, the need to develop skills and mechanisms for employee involvement and participation in the widest sense will increase.

This setting is consistent with Greiner's analysis that, in Phase 5, organizations would face a crisis resulting from the problems of 'psychological saturation' of employees who become emotionally and physically exhausted by the intensity of teamwork and the heavy pressure for innovative solutions. The extent to which this is with us is reflected in the attention currently being given to stress at work, and its high costs in terms of levels of absence, 'burnout' and early retirement among employees.

Through this one can also see the emergence of new forms of organizational structure. Particularly worth noting is that which Charles Handy (1989) terms federalism. In this he sees the means to combining organizational groupings through shared identity, autonomy and cooperation. This can result in businesses getting

the best of both worlds—the size which gives them the clout in the marketplace and in the financial centres, as well as some economies of scale, and the small unit size which gives them the flexibility which they need, as well as the sense of community for which individuals increasingly hanker (p.93).

The essence of federalism is the pursuit of effectiveness through a 'coming together' quite distinct from the traditional decentralization model in which the centre retains overall control. With federalism, the centre's power is determined by the organizational groupings. Thus its capacity to make decisions, direct and control are constrained mainly to strategic issues and its influence largely determined by its capacity to advise, negotiate and coordinate.

The shift to a federalist structure is a fundamental one and so too are the training implications. Handy highlights the position beautifully in his observation that:

The federal organization is not only different in its form and shape, it is also culturally different, it requires a different set of attitudes from those who seek to run it and from those who seek to manage it and from those who are managed. This is the discontinuity which matters—not the change in structure but the change in philosophy (p.99).

This aspect of culture and its associated training implications is the subject of the chapter which follows.

Note

1 See, for example, the British Institute of Management's series of publications, including:
   Alban Metcalfe, B. and N. Nicholson (1984) *The Career Development of British Managers.*
   Coulson, C. and T. Coe (1991) *The Flat Organisation: Philosophy and Practice.*
   Peppercorn, G. and G. Skoulding (1987) *Management Profile in British Industry.*
   Wheatley, M. (1991) *The Future of Middle Management.*

References

Chandler Jr, A.D. (1962) *Strategy and Structure: Chapters in the History of American Industrial Enterprise*, Cambridge, MA: MIT Press.
Greiner, L.E. (1972) 'Evolution and revolution as organizations grow', *Harvard Business Review on Management*, July–August.
Handy, C. (1989) *The Age of Unreason*, London: Business Books.

5 Culture

The significance of culture for the trainer

The issues discussed under the heading of structure in the previous chapter have also been reflected in the great concern and attention that has been given to organizational culture during the past five to ten years on both sides of the Atlantic. In the process, much attention has also been devoted to learning from Japan. As a result, so much has now been written on the subject that it is difficult to know where to start in terms of providing an overview. At the same time, it is probably fair to say that whereas much progress has been made in terms of understanding the issues and their significance, major problems have been and continue to be experienced in trying to introduce cultural change within organizations.

Many would argue that training—or lack of it—lies at the heart of these problems. Trainers have, therefore, particularly good reason to develop their role and skills in this area. This chapter therefore seeks to set out a broad framework for understanding organizational culture, the training issues that it raises, and some basic tools of analysis which might be helpful in the process.

Primarily, the study of an organization's culture is concerned with seeking to understand deep-seated beliefs about the way work should be organized and the manner in which authority should be exercised. In turn, this manifests itself in the kinds of people employed, career structures and aspirations, systems of reward, both material and psychological, management style and methods of control.

It is for these reasons that organizations so often look and feel different, appeal to different kinds of people and provide contexts in which some people thrive and others wilt. Much of the conflict that surrounds change in organizations can be seen as a struggle between competing cultures. Thus, besides being the product of people's behaviour, organization culture also shapes it and the way in which the organization copes with its external environment.

The importance of this was captured by Allen Kennedy at Mckinsey and Terrence Deal at Harvard in their exploration of the connection between corporate values and national cultures. In the process, they noted the absence of relationships among variables that organization theory said should be related. This led them to the view that 'structure and strategy may be more symbolic than substantive' and the hypothesis that 'the companies that did best over the long haul were those that believed in something' (Deal and Kennedy, 1982, p.6). From their subsequent analysis of nearly 80 companies they found that:

—Of all the companies surveyed, only about one third (twenty-five to be precise) had clearly articulated beliefs.

—Of this third, a surprising two-thirds had qualitative beliefs, or values, such as 'IBM means service.' The other third had financially oriented goals that were widely understood.

—Of the eighteen companies with qualitative beliefs, all were uniformly out-standing performers; we could find no correlations of any relevance among the other companies—some did okay, some poorly, others had their ups and downs. We characterized the consistently high performers as strong culture companies (p.7).

The unanswered questions were, of course, to do with the distinctions between different degrees of success, how such values were acquired and how they were transmitted through the organization. The search to find the answers fuelled the explosion of interest in corporate cultures and the associated value systems (see Figure 5.1).

Strong cultures associated with successful companies

- They stand for something—that is, they have a clear and explicit philosophy about how they aim to conduct their business.
- Management pays a great deal of attention to shaping and fine-tuning these values to conform to the economic and business environment of the company and to communicating them to the organization.
- These values are known and shared by all the people who work for the company—from the lowliest production worker right through to the ranks of senior management.

Weak cultures associated with companies in trouble

- Weak cultures have no clear values or beliefs about how to succeed in their business; or
- They have many such beliefs but cannot agree among themselves on which are the most important; or
- Different parts of the company have fundamentally different beliefs.
- The heroes (role models) of the culture are destructive or disruptive and don't build upon any common understanding about what is important.
- The rituals of day-to-day life are either disorganized—with everybody doing their own thing—or downright contradictory—with the left hand working at cross-purposes.

Figure 5.1　*Strong versus weak cultures*
(Source: T. Deal and A. Kennedy, Corporate Cultures, © 1982, Addison-Wesley Publishing Company, Inc. Reprinted with permission of the publisher)

Issues for the trainer

Culture has clear implications for training. At one level these range from initial socialization and induction of new members into the organization, through job skills training—to transmit the values attached to the ways of doing things—to career planning and development. At another, it opens up the whole area of training for organizational effectiveness. In practical terms, the trainer needs to get to grips with:

- Understanding the organization's predominant beliefs
- Identifying the sort of skills that are called for to be effective within it
- Assessing the extent to which they are held and shared throughout the organization
- Designing and implementing training, not only to ensure their transmission but also in a way which is consistent with them
- Identifying changes in the organization's beliefs and providing appropriate training to suit
- Examining the effect of the organization's culture on productivity

To put this in perspective, an example which comes to mind is that of an educational establishment. Like many others in its field, it was steeped in many years of tradition and history. Its staff, many of whom had given very long service, had established what many regarded amounted to 'property rights' in their jobs and ways of working. In contrast, the top management group were relatively very new, not just to the organization but also to both the sort of work involved and level of responsibility required of them. Indeed, they even liked to refer to themselves as 'the new team'.

Despite rapidly growing student numbers, a feature which characterized many parts of the education sector, budgetary constraints and underfunding over many years provided an acutely difficult climate in which to manage from day to day, let alone develop and introduce the long-term strategic change. The union was enjoying a level of support not previously experienced and there were distinct signs tantamount to anarchy among an increasing number of staff. For their part, the new management were displaying increasing signs of frustration at their almost total inability to bring the organization into line with a much harsher economic climate and a more competitive world.

In what seemed an almost last-gasp effort to bring about a change in attitudes, management called a meeting of senior staff to identify and consider barriers to change. The start was not perfect, much time being spent waiting for members of the teaching faculties who had not only not replied to the invitations to attend but had also gone off on their extended summer vacation, in accordance with 'longstanding custom and practice'. It was perhaps unfortunate, too, that management called the meeting on what some administration staff rather affectionately referred to as 'poets day' (push off early, tomorrow's Saturday), thus limiting attendance still further.

To cut short what is in danger of becoming a long story, the discussions which did take place led to the conclusion that one of the major problems facing the organization was what effectively amounted to two competing cultures. More than this, since management had failed to articulate and gain acceptance of their plans for the strategic development of the organization and the need for change, staff felt that they had a real and vested interest in resisting it—an imperfect present being seen as better than the future seen to be on offer.

Underlying this, however, could be seen to be a highly destructive pattern of behaviour which characterized the organization and its process of decision making. In a nutshell, a lack of confidence of staff in management provided a basis for resisting change. More than this, for many it had also become 'fun' to resist change—first they could deride management for getting into a mess, then they could stand back and enjoy watching them trying to get out of it.

Whatever the fundamental strengths, resources and skills this particular organization might possess, whether it has the capacity to survive intact on a long-term view would seem questionable. What is certain, though, is that if it is to do so, huge commitments to training in terms of time, money and energy will be needed in order to create a shared and workable culture and system of values sufficient to transform the organization into an effective whole.

Tools of analysis

A sound starting point is to consider the various elements and determinants of culture, i.e.:

- The business environment of which it is a part and to which it has to adapt
- Strategy and structure, which reflect not only the organization's response to its environment, but also its values
- The values which represent the basic beliefs of the organization in terms of what it stands for and the way in which it conducts its affairs
- Role models, i.e. those individuals who personify the organization's values
- The rituals which reflect the expected behaviour of employees
- The reward systems, in both a material and psychological sense, and which reinforce through both positive and negative means the behaviour expected of employees
- The training system which, using the term in its widest sense, transmits the organization's culture to its members and provides for their socialization

Trainers are also likely to find that the early analysis developed by Roger Harrison (1972) provides a good example of the ways in which these various aspects combine together to form different cultures. In essence, his conceptual framework postulates four organization ideologies:

1 Power orientation
2 Role orientation

3 Task orientation
4 Person orientation

Although these orientations will seldom be found as 'pure types', most organizations will tend towards one or other of them. These various orientations are discussed below.

Power orientation   An organization that is power oriented can be recognized by both its external and internal behaviour. Externally, it attempts to dominate its environment. At its extreme this may include markets, products, territory, access to resources and even violation of legal requirements.

To the outside world such organizations, especially if they are large, will sometimes be perceived to be run by colourful, larger-than-life personalities. Internally, things may be seen rather differently. For example, the predominant management style may be experienced as one of striving to maintain control over subordinates with an apparent disregard of human values and social responsibility. Less extreme forms of power culture are often found in smaller businesses of the traditional family type and can be recognized by a management style based on benevolent authority.

Role orientation   In contrast to the autocracy prevalent within the power-oriented organization, those with a role culture can be recognized by their preoccupation with regulation and legitimacy. They are likely to place a strong emphasis on hierarchy and status, defined rights and entitlements, and the resolution of conflict through the application of agreements, rules and procedures. They are likely to appeal to those who value rationality, impersonality and compliance with procedures rather than flexibility, adaptability and responsiveness to change.

Task orientation   Task-oriented organizations can be recognized by the way in which they reveal an overriding sense of purpose. Such organizations place a high value on task accomplishment and its contribution to the organization's overall aims. In turn, organization structure is shaped and modified in accordance with the task to be accomplished.

It is perhaps analogous with the rather overused but effective image of a football team where the needs of the moment determine how the team adapts its formation and activities. Contrast this with the cricketing team, where, when fielding, players have defined and relatively fixed positions and roles, or, when batting, are mostly to be found in the pavilion!

Person orientation   In contrast to the other three types, the person-oriented organization exists primarily to serve the interests of its members. Authority is barely visible, since the basis of the organization is individual responsibility, competence, example and concern for others. Such organizations place a relatively low value on profitability and growth as a criterion for success. Instead, the emphasis will be on personal satisfaction, personal learning and developing supportive relationships.

Structural connections, strengths and weaknesses

In a general sense, these different orientations can be seen to dovetail nicely with our understanding of the behavioural consequences which result from different forms of structure. For example:

- The power-oriented organization is not well suited to flexible response, effective information processing and decision making. The reason for this is that, since decisions are made at the top, the information needed may be subject to time lags, selectivity and manipulation as it is passed up the organization. Where it does possess strengths, subject to the quality of those exercising control, is in its ability to operate with few rules and procedures, enabling it to respond swiftly to perceived threats in its environment.
- The role-oriented organization may have the merits of stability and consistency but is also likely to suffer from lack of responsiveness— not least to its customers—due to its reliance on established roles and reporting relationships. Rapid change may render established procedures irrelevant to the real needs of the organization for adaptability and information channels may become overloaded. In consequence, decision making can be severely impaired.
- Both the task- and person-oriented organizations have strengths in dealing with changing environments due to the relative ease of communication resulting from their flatter structures and scope for more cooperative working relationships. However, the need to obtain consent and commitment from members can be time consuming. Additionally, the requirement to reorder goals and priorities, particularly when the 'going gets tough', can be a source of conflict between individuals and sections of the organization, who may be reluctant to sacrifice their personal goals. Thus, in a sense, it can be seen that overcoming the problem of managing depth is exchanged for that of managing breadth.

In reviewing an organization's culture Harrison (1972) concludes that the critical factor to assess is the degree of viability of the organization. Thus, from an internal perspective, an organization might be said to be viable when the people within it want and need the prescribed incentives and satisfactions on offer. Externally, viability can be seen to be the level of consistency between the culture of the organization and the wider environment of which it is really no more than a microcosm.

Keys to understanding

The interconnection between structure and culture is to be expected since, at heart, both have a common root in being concerned with the way in which authority should be exercised. In the UK, Charles Handy (1985) can be seen to have developed and popularized these ideas in his conceptualization of the Gods of Management. In doing so he made a clear and important shift in his consideration of culture being more a product of values than structure—a theme to which he has returned and developed in *The Age of Unreason* (1989).

Yet, despite all that has been written about corporate culture since the concept caught and held the imagination of the business world during the 1980s, it retains an elusive quality. This makes it particularly difficult for trainers to get to grips with. In its own way, it is as slippery as soap in the bath! Although directing his remarks to managers, Gareth Morgan (1989) captures this situation beautifully and in a way that is directly relevant to trainers when he observes:

As one tries to look at the organization with fresh eyes, one can see the intangible 'social glue' that holds everything together: how the language, norms, values, rituals, myths, stories and daily routines form part of a coherent 'reality' that lends shape to how and what people do as they go about their work.

In understanding this 'social glue' (which like all glue sometimes does not stick as well as it might, producing a fragmented or divided 'culture') other ways of thinking about culture might be appropriate.

For example try thinking about the corporate culture as an iceberg. Recognize that what you see on the surface is based on a much deeper reality. Recognize that the visible elements of the culture may be sustained by all kinds of hidden values, beliefs, ideologies and assumptions—questioned and unquestioned, conscious and unconscious. As a manager, (*or trainer*) recognize that it may not be possible to change the surface without changing what lies below.

Or try thinking about the corporate culture as an onion. Recognize that it has different layers. Recognize that one can penetrate beneath the rituals, ceremonies and symbolic routines to discover inner layers of mythology, folklore, hopes and dreams that eventually lead to the innermost values and assumptions that lend meaning to the outward aspect of the culture. Recognize that to change the culture in any significant way it is necessary to address and perhaps change the values that lie at the core.

Or try thinking about the corporate culture as an umbrella. Look for the overarching values and visions that unite, or are capable of uniting, the individuals and groups working under the umbrella. Recognize that one's ability to mobilize or change any organization may depend upon finding the umbrella that can unite potentially divergent individuals, groups and sub-cultures in pursuit of a shared vision of reality.

Whatever one's favoured metaphor—whether iceberg, onion, umbrella or sticky glue—it seems important to remember that there's more to corporate culture than meets the eye. Just as the culture of a country tends to be shaped and sustained by deeply held core values and beliefs, so too in the corporate world. Changing corporate culture is not like changing a suit of clothes. One can change surface appearances, e.g. by giving the corporation a new image, introducing staff picnics, and espousing new philosophies and beliefs. But to have significant and lasting impact, basic values also have to change (pp. 157–8).

This description reflects how, in essence, the key to examining an organization's culture is to seek to understand its values, particularly relative to the exercise of authority and, in turn, their relevance to its context. It also illustrates how, given the diversity of human behaviour, this is easier said than done. Accordingly, simple frameworks applied with flexibility and discretion can be as helpful as diagnostic tools than more complicated approaches.

For these reasons, models and approaches such as those of Harrison and Morgan are extremely helpful as starting points. They have stood the test of time well, are readily understood by managers and provide tools for the trainer in the process.

These frameworks also possess the same sort of dialectic quality as Greiner's model of organization development, discussed in the previous chapter. They are therefore able to accommodate the contradictions so apparent in organizational life. Besides giving insights into organization functioning, they also encourage new ways of looking at organizations. In turn, they can be used to illustrate how every decision not only risks creating its own unwanted side effects but also tends to produce movement in the direction opposite to that intended.

Identifying these contradictions is essential to the process of recognizing the need for cultural change and the design of effective and consistent training strategies to implement it. In turn, the ability to manage such contradictions and change is a fundamental skill requirement for managers. Without it, they will not be able to manage the integration of the different parts of the business.

References

Deal, T.E. and A.A. Kennedy (1982) *Corporate Cultures: The Rites and Rituals of Corporate Life*, Reading, M.A: Addison-Wesley.

Handy, C. (1985) *Gods of Management*, London: Pan.

Handy, C. (1989) *The Age of Unreason*, London: Business Books.

Harrison, R. (1972) 'How to describe your organization', *Harvard Business Review*, Sept–Oct.

Morgan, G. (1989) *Creative Organization Theory*, Beverly Hills, CA: Sage.

Conclusion to Part Two

In order to identify the overall training needs of an organization the trainer needs to be able to form an overview of its strategy, structure and culture. The reason for this is that these interlocking components determine the needs for skills and training throughout the organization, while also reflecting the attitudes, knowledge and skills of management. Intervention at this level therefore gives a unique opportunity to review the skills possessed and needed by the entire workforce.

The increasing rate of organizational change provides an example of how important the assessment process is. It underpins the goal of improving competitiveness through the strengthening of market positions, or developing new ones, on the one hand, and minimizing costs, on the other. Such changes are dependent upon the careful assessment of training needs and development of skills in the management of change.

In addition to functional or operational training, staff also need training to understand the purposes of the organization, how it works and their contribution to it. Without it, the increasing pressures faced by operating management and employees will result not only in a failure to achieve the strategic and operational goals of the organization but also the long-term and deep-seated cost of dissatisfied employees.

At this stage some questions you could consider might include:

What is your organization's strategy?
—Has it been translated into terms of skills?
—If not, what sort of barriers need to be surmounted to bring it about?
Does the organization structure work in terms of:
—Being responsive to the demands put upon it?
—Providing wanted career opportunities?
How would you describe your organization's culture?
—Does it hinder or foster productivity?
—What sort of skills are required to work within it and are they provided?

PART THREE

Financial appraisal

Introduction

Many trainers reading this book will already be familiar with basic financial statements, i.e. the balance sheet, profit and loss statement and sources and application of funds. Where they may be less surefooted is in the application of the information contained within them to the training function. This part therefore sets out to provide an explanation of the 'training connection' and their use as a tool for analysis.

For those unfamiliar with financial statements or wishing to refresh their memories, Appendix 1 includes a brief and practical review. Chapter 10 also contains an analysis of the accounts relating to ABCO, the company upon which the case study in Part Five is based. For those wanting more, the suggestions for further reading at the end of the book should be helpful.

So, accounts are for trainers—but why? First, the financial structure and results of an organization can be used to reflect its performance, strengths, weaknesses and potential. This is because, although it is all too rarely appreciated, accounts are in fact measures of human behaviour and performance. If you have any doubts about this, reflect for a moment upon your reaction to receiving details of your individual account from your bank or credit card company . . . Second, for a business, the various financial statements reflect the decision-making skills of management in allocating resources and those of the entire workforce in making the best use of them. Together they reflect the organization's skills and success in the achievement of its objectives. Third, it is only by understanding the financial position of a business that trainers can develop profitable training strategies. And, in the long run, regardless of how high the quality of the products or services and the commitment of the workforce, the survival of a business is dependent upon the generation of profits. Fourth, understanding accounts enables trainers to make better decisions. It helps them to decide, for example, the appropriate level and allocation of training budgets, as well as the priorities within them. Thus trainers can contribute not only to the financial performance of a business but also to its capacity to survive. Fifth, accounts provide an excellent starting point for the trainer to get to grips with the business and generate hard evidence as a basis for arguing the case for training. In its own way, this is akin to the sporting analogy in which there is a basic assumption that, providing performance is consistently measured, improvements in it can be achieved.

Underlying all of these aspects is the point that, although financial accounts do not provide a total picture of the health of a business, they are the only quantifiable picture that is available. They are also, as John Elliott, Director of the Institute of Manpower Studies, puts it: '. . . In the common language of the client. With that language trainers have to be able to understand, analyse and make their case for scarce funds. In the parlance of management theorists, the accounts are also a brilliant conceptual framework' (Elliott, 1991).

Reference

Elliott, J. (1991) 'Training for profit—a review', *Transition*, January.

6 Ratio analysis—a tool for the trainer

Training and accounts—the vital connection

Although it was more than twenty years ago, I can remember the day that I first made the connection between financial accounts and training as if it were yesterday. I had spent some time reviewing the commercial training arrangements in one of Britain's large electrical businesses and was due to make my report to its Commercial Director.

As I drove through the early morning freshness of a sunny day in May, I felt a sense of tingling excitement at what lay in store. Perhaps it was fuelled, too, by listening to Dr Michael Argyle being interviewed on radio about his latest research findings into eye contact, the direction of gaze, dominance and submission (see Argyle, 1972). Little did I know of the profound significance that Argyle's advice to listeners would hold for me within the hour.

I didn't 'arrive' at the Commercial Director's office, I was 'wheeled' into it and greeted with the words 'Well, Mr Darling, what do you think *you* can do to help us with *our* training?' At best, the welcome seemed tough, and at worst, aggressive—there was I standing, back to the door, almost as green as they come, having to confront this 'very big cheese', sitting in a black leather swivel-back chair behind a huge rosewood desk. For a moment I really wouldn't have minded if I had fallen through a hole in the floor—it would have rendered unnecessary momentary considerations of such issues as flight or fight!

I am sure Dr Argyle would have been thrilled to know how quickly I absorbed his advice. Fixing my eye on my assailant, I found myself saying words to the effect of 'Well, Mr . . ., I can see that you do a lot of good training here. What I don't understand is, if it's so good (as you seem to be suggesting), how come the company's got such a large over-draft and such heavy borrowings?'

The silence which followed was awful, but was redeemed at last by the immortal words: 'Good Lord, pull up a chair.' I was in! By putting a pound sign in front of training—as opposed, all too often, to after it—I had transformed, for this particular person, the notion of training from being a cost to that of an objective investment.

This was an important moment for me, for it rendered redundant the then (and still) far too common managerial argument that training is too expensive, or just involves sending individuals on money-wasting courses. Instead it offered the exciting prospect of developing an approach to selling training on the basis of identifying those areas of a business which were unprofitable as a direct means of improving efficiency and results.

For me, this early moment sowed the seeds of the 'Training for Profit' approach as a means of shifting the focus of training from traditional approaches based upon individual or group training needs to one which could provide a much sharper focus on the application of skills. However, simply identifying profitable training opportunities is not enough—as with any investment, there are opportunity costs involved and which need to be taken into account.

The real significance of such costs was bought home to me, most painfully, following an assignment in a bottling hall of a large wines and spirits company. With a colleague to assist, many hours, indeed weeks, were spent carrying out the most thorough assessment of training needs I have ever witnessed. Working back from theoretical to actual outputs, we identified tremendous opportunities for investing in training in order to increase output and productivity and reduce wastage and 'lost time'. In the process, we profiled the skills of the workforce and identified the shortcomings of the training system.

In short, it was a super job. The Production Director liked it, so did his staff, including those responsible for training. Compared with the benefits involved, the set-up costs were minimal. So why did it, for the most part, remain on the shelf?

I got my answer, when I went to see the Managing Director. 'Listen, sonny,' he said, 'the problem here is not production, it's sales. We're expecting a serious downturn in our revenues.'

Despite being many years ago, this experience still hurts. Like most trainers, I'm sure, I hate committing myself to a piece of work and finding it disregarded. That one gets paid for the job doesn't matter. The issue is one of misdirected effort—and, as in this case, opportunity cost. Just think what might have been achieved by investing the equivalent amount of time and effort in the company's marketing and sales operation!

This example reflects clearly the need for an overall approach. Only by doing so can one be sure of directing one's efforts and training investment to best advantage. It is within this context that ratio analysis really comes into its own.

Uses of ratio analysis

One of the limitations of financial statements is that the figures, when looked at in isolation, may provide only a very general indication of financial position of the business.[1] However, by comparing them with other figures as a percentage or ratio and setting them against similar figures for previous accounting periods, trends become apparent. As a result, areas of particular need and opportunity can be highlighted as a basis for planning specifically related training.

From the trainer's viewpoint the techniques provide the basis to:

- Understand the effectiveness of the organization
- Allow comparisons to be made between one year's performance and another's
- Contrast one organization with another as a basis for seeking to understand differences in performance
- Identify areas where performance may need to be improved
- Assess potential training contributions
- Relate training strategy to organizational strategy, i.e. serve as a basis for assessing training needs and developing training plans across the organization
- Control training investment and evaluate its effectiveness

Conceptual foundations

There are a number of approaches to ratio analysis, though basically they are very similar. One of the most widely known is the Pyramid method, developed by the Centre for InterFirm Comparison. To use this approach, it is first necessary to identify those factors upon which success depends and to devise the most appropriate measurements for monitoring them.

For most organizations the starting point for analysis is the return on capital employed or return on assets, since these represent fundamental indicators of profitability (see below) and reflect the extent to which an organization generates returns proportionate to the resources invested. Having selected the ratio which best measures overall success, further ratios can then be chosen to examine and explain in greater detail the principal ratios. Thus the analysis progresses from the general to the particular. As it does so, the ratios build up systematically into an integrated set that can be used to quantify the contribution which the various parts of an organization make towards overall success.

Figure 6.1 shows a typical pyramid for a manufacturing company; the same principles (but a different set of ratios) can be used to analyse the performance of any organization, whether it is a private company, a public utility or a professional partnership.

According to the level of analysis required, a wide range of ratios can be applied. For instance, 20 to 30 ratios will often be sufficient to form an overview of a business. A complete analysis of a company or a division within it could involve many interlocking ratios. By applying these tools of analysis, the trainer is able to address a very wide range of issues. These are listed in Chapter 2 but are repeated here for simplicity:

1 What is the picture reflected in the trends over a period of years? For example,
   —What is happening to levels of profitability?

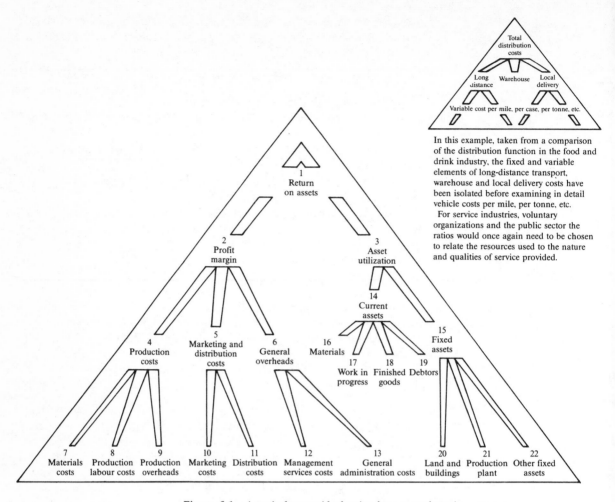

Figure 6.1   *A typical pyramid of ratios for a manufacturing company*
                  (Source: The Centre for Interfirm Comparison. Used with permission
                  of the CIC)

—Is the business growing or contracting?
—Is productivity rising or falling?
—Is liquidity and solvency increasing or decreasing?
2 What is the overall picture indicated by the figures for the current
   year? For example,
   —Is there sufficient liquidity, profit and capital?
   —How strong or weak is the business in financial terms?
   —Has it borrowing potential?
   —To what extent is it taking too much credit or failing to control
      debtors or stock levels?
3 What is the gap between current performance and that planned for
   the future?

The trainer can then go on to ask further questions about the
implications of the information revealed. For example:

- What questions does this raise about the company's skills in developing and implementing policies, procedures and methods of operating? Does management appear to be in control? To what extent might issues of decision making, organization and job design be involved?
- Where do the major strengths and weaknesses, problems and opportunities appear to lie? What would seem to be areas for priority action? What sort of benefits might be expected to result from tackling them? What would be the likely impact on profitability?
- What does it suggest about the general level of skills in managing the business and those in operating its component parts and major functions? Does it suggest that management is well informed and acts upon the information available to it?
- What are the possible implications and priorities for exploiting areas where skills exist and remedying deficiencies?

Getting started

Essential to understanding ratio analysis is an appreciation of overall management performance ratios, the starting point for which is the company's return on capital employed:

$$\frac{\text{Profit before tax}}{\text{Capital employed}}$$

Capital employed is equivalent to the sum of fixed assets and net current assets (working capital).[2] It is this which provides the context for understanding the subsequent ratios relating to the operating and financial management of the business. It is important, also, to understand that the return on capital employed is a function of both the profit on sales and the number of times that capital is turned over:

$$\frac{\text{Profit before tax}}{\text{Sales}} \qquad \frac{\text{Sales}}{\text{Capital employed}}$$

Thus a company turning over its capital twice a year and making 10 per cent on sales is earning a 20 per cent return on capital. If it were turning it over three times a year and making 15 per cent in the process it would be earning 45 per cent.

Therefore, in seeking to improve its performance, a business can pursue a mix of strategies ranging from improving either the turnover of capital, or the margin on sales, or both. In practice, it is therefore important that these two ratios are considered together.

Whereas the return on sales ratio provides an overall indication of the company's success at managing its expenditure (for example, on production, marketing, administration and research and development) within its revenue, turnover of capital employed reflects the relationship between sales and capital. The significance of this should not be missed, for it provides the key to identifying areas in need of improvement and developing strategies for doing so. For example, from this basic starting point it is possible to form an initial view on the need for controlling costs, managing prices or developing sales.

Factors for consideration

In carrying out this sort of analysis it needs to be borne in mind that there will be wide variations between different companies' performance ratios. For instance, a merchanting business or a retailer of fast-moving consumer goods might be expected to turn over its capital at a much faster rate than, say, a railway, shipbuilder or manufacturer of capital goods. This is because of the relative differences in levels of investment in fixed assets and working capital required to engage in different activities. Similarly, a service business such as a finance house, consultancy, advertising agency or dancing school, where the assets are primarily people and therefore rarely included in the balance sheet, might be expected to achieve returns on capital very much higher than one characterized by high levels of investment in fixed assets.

It may also be observed that investment increases in 'steps', rather than a 'straight line' (for example, when an airline expands or renews its fleet). This means that there may be times when a business is experiencing a period of sustained growth, when 'super-profits' can be achieved, i.e. between the steps.

A further important variant will be the return on capital objective set by management and the extent to which 'planning the balance sheet' is seen as an important activity. In this there is an element of profitability being not just a cost of doing or staying in business but also an 'attitude of mind'—clearly a concept of great significance for the trainer, in that it offers the potential of a self-fulfilling and circular process. Thus a business seeking a return of 50 per cent on capital might be expected to display a very different set of attitudes and behaviour than businesses in the same market seeking returns of 20 per cent or 100 per cent.

Although the level of profits regarded as necessary to maintain and develop a business is essentially a management decision, in the long run every business needs to generate real returns on capital in order to stay in business and justify the investment of its owners. Thus, in times of high inflation or high risk, increasing returns on capital are desirable. From a training perspective, the concern is to assess the extent to which the adequacy or inadequacy of the return is reflective of training needs and opportunities. Where no return on capital objective is set, this often in itself implies training needs in both business planning and financial management skills.

As a general rule, research findings show that earning a healthy profit margin is more important in the achievement of a good return on capital employed than attaining a high turnover of capital.[3] This does not mean, however, that the importance of capital turnover should be overlooked. Depending upon the particular circumstances of a business, or trends in its markets, it can be critical—for instance, when it is:

- Poor in absolute terms or relative to the organization's past performance or to its competitors
- Used as a competitive strategy directed towards gaining market share or maintaining profitability in adverse market conditions when margins are under pressure.

It is also worth noting at this point that achieving a high profit margin tends to result from an appropriate balance between costs and revenues, rather than minimizing costs per unit of output or solely maximizing revenue per unit through high prices. Similarly, in the management of production and the management of assets it is the balance struck between results achieved and both resources used and resources available that reflects success.

Thus the balance between costs and revenues, assets and output tends to be more important than the absolute level of items such as labour costs per employee or capital investment per employee. In turn, the balance and results achieved reflect the policies, practices and skills of the organization's management.

Conclusion

The return on capital ratio provides a good starting point for analysing the overall performance of a business. Thereafter the return on sales and turnover of capital ratios can be used to form an initial view, at least, of whether attention is likely to be needed to be given to achieving improvements in sales profitability, turnover, or both.

Even at this early stage, consideration of the size of the gap between what is required and what is being achieved can provide a 'feel' that allows a perspective to be formed on whether the needs facing the business are primarily for improvement, maintenance or development and the extent to which they are of a short- or long-term priority. These perceptions in turn serve as the basis for considering training strategy.

A point which needs to be reiterated is that, in applying ratio analysis, the purpose is to examine the organization as a whole, even though the main training priorities may lie in one particular area. It is therefore important to conduct the assessment by proceeding from the general to the particular, from overall objectives and measures of performance to the reasons for lack of (or unsatisfactory) results. The structure for extending this analysis is provided in the chapter which follows.

Finally, as a tool for assessing and reflecting the performance, strengths, weaknesses and potential of almost every part and function of an organization, ratio analysis is central to the Training for Profit approach. Applying these techniques to measuring changes in the financial results and structure of a business provides a logical and measurable basis to reflect the interrelationship between the organization's activities and their contribution to overall performance. The key to the training connection is the likelihood that differences in performance are rooted in differences in management policies and practices—and hence not just their own skills but those of the entire workforce.

Notes

1 Further limitations and *caveats* are included in Appendix 1.
2 Where assets include those not used in the trading process—for example, intangibles such as goodwill and brands—until accountancy standards become clearer, it is generally better to exclude them and use the rate of return on net operating assets as a basis for assessing overall performance. For profit, the pre-tax figure should be used since taxation can vary from year to year for reasons which may not be directly related to the year's trading activities. Similarly, where profits accrue from non-trading activities, these should be deducted and the figure for operating profits used.
3 See, for example, *Management Policies and Practices, and Business Performance*, A Report by the Centre for InterFirm Comparison, 1977; or *Performance Comparisons: Analysis of Key Financial Ratios*, Lloyds Bowmaker, 1989; or 'The European Top 500', *Financial Times*, 1992 or *Fortune 500*.

Reference

Argyle, M. (1972) *The Psychology of Interpersonal Behaviour*, Harmondsworth: Penguin.

Suggested further reading

Allen, D. (1991) *Strategic Financial Management in Practice*, Financial Times Management Reports.
Business Ratios: a new guide to interpretation, ICC.
Cooper, R. and R.S. Kaplan (1988) 'Measure costs right: make the right decisions', *Harvard Business Review*, September–October, pp. 96–103.
Parker, R.H. (1988) *Understanding Company Financial Statements*, 3rd edition, Harmondsworth: Penguin.
Pendlebury, M. (ed.) (1989) *Management Accounting in the Public Sector*, London: Heinemann/CIMA.
Scapens, R.W. (1991) *Management Accounting: A Review of Recent Developments*, 2nd edition, London: Macmillan.

7 Getting to grips: operating, cost and financial management performance ratios

Introduction

Having examined the overall management performance ratios a more detailed analysis of financial statements can be made. For training purposes, although the distinction is somewhat artificial, these secondary management performance ratios can usefully be considered under the headings of:

1 Operating performance
2 Elements of cost
3 Financial performance

Whereas operating performance ratios provide a focus on profitability, those for financial performance can be used to reflect the financial strength and stability of the business.

Operating performance ratios

Sales growth

Sales growth can be expressed as a percentage of the year-on-year increase in sales. By comparing it with the rate of inflation and relative price indices, an indication of real sales performance and the ability to pass on changes in prices can be obtained. Additionally, comparisons with competitors may suggest the level of success being achieved in maintaining and developing market share. Where the rate of growth is lower than the rate of inflation, it may reflect a lack of success or that the market for the company's products and services is declining.

Return on operating assets

$$\frac{\text{Operating profit}}{\text{Operating assets}}$$

This ratio provides a refinement on the return on capital concept. It gives an indication of the effectiveness of the organization in terms of the investment decisions it has made and its success in planning and controlling its activities.

Turnover of assets

$$\frac{\text{Sales}}{\text{Operating assets}}$$

The rate of asset turnover indicates the intensity with which the organization is using its assets. Hence it can provide an indication of trends in the utilization of capacity. However, the ratio can be misleading, since it may be unduly influenced by changes in material costs. Where this is the case it is better to use the ratio of added value to operating assets, i.e. deduct the cost of materials from sales. A further refinement of this is provided by dividing added value by fixed assets. It can be used to determine whether changes in asset utilization are due primarily to changes in the effectiveness of the use of fixed or current assets.

Gross profit margin and added value

$$\frac{\text{Gross profit}}{\text{Sales}} \qquad \frac{\text{Added value}}{\text{Sales}}$$

Whereas the net profit margin suggests the proportion of sales revenue remaining after expenses, the gross profit margin excludes non-production costs (for example, those of marketing and administration). Key questions to consider are whether the margin appears to be sufficient for the needs of the business and the extent to which improved overall returns are more likely to result from focusing upon it or looking elsewhere.

Changes in the gross profit margin can reflect changes in market competitiveness and the ability to pass on costs. It can also reflect the ability of management to control the costs of production. The gross profit margin tends to be more stable than the net profit margin, since a relatively high proportion of the costs involved are likely to be those that vary directly with sales.

Where material costs represent a high proportion of total costs, the use and expression of added value as a percentage of sales instead of gross profit may provide a sharper focus. It can also be used to reflect the extent to which increases in sales revenue are being eaten up by higher materials costs.

Added value per employee and per pound of wages

$$\frac{\text{Added value}}{\text{No. of employees}} \qquad \frac{\text{Added value}}{\text{£wages}}$$

Dividing added value (i.e. sales less material costs) by the number of employees provides a broad indicator of productivity. Since this discounts the undue influence of changes in raw materials prices it is generally superior to that of simply measuring sales per employee.

Even more pertinent is the calculation of added value per pound of wages. It can be used to show the extent to which gains in productivity per employee have been passed on in wage rates or applied elsewhere in the business.

Capital investment per employee

$$\frac{\text{Fixed assets}}{\text{No. of employees}}$$

This can provide a broad measure of the capital intensity of the business. However, in its interpretation all the caveats in valuing fixed assets and changes to depreciation policies need to be borne in mind (see Appendix 1). It can be useful to calculate separate ratios for capital equipment and land and buildings.

When forming an overview of an organization's performance, this is often an appropriate point at which to break off and talk over the questions raised, including any training implications, directly with the line managers concerned. If, however, further information is required before doing so, this will need to be related to the specific issues involved. In these circumstances the range of analysis which might be applied is unlimited. In practice, however, carrying out further ratio analysis in order to understand better the main elements of cost is likely to prove the most fruitful.

Main elements of cost

For most purposes, a good starting point is to focus on the balance between and trends in material costs, wage costs, and the expenses relating to manufacturing, research and development, selling and distribution, and administration, all expressed as a percentage of sales. The picture provided by these figures will often give a good indication of the extent to which costs appear to be under control. Are they, for example, increasing or decreasing? How is the balance between them changing and why should this be so? Do they suggest consistency, or are they 'all over the place'? Additionally, the value of their respective contributions can be considered as a means of deciding priorities for further investigation. Where adverse trends in the main elements of cost are apparent, there is clearly a need for a closer examination.

It is typically from this analysis of the main elements of cost that areas for training needs and opportunities are most readily clarified. More than this, since managements are so often concerned to reduce costs, it is an area of great appeal to them—and particularly useful if one of the needs is to create a greater awareness among managers of the need for training and the benefits which can accrue.

By way of example, in a production context, this sort of analysis might lead to consideration of actual output relative to theoretical or planned output. In turn, the analysis of under performance might focus on:

- 'Lost time'—for example, setting, change-overs, breakdowns, material

shortages, below 'experienced worker standard' performance, absence, accidents, disputes, etc.
- 'Scrap and rework', including, for example, raw materials, work in progress and finished goods

Within a sales operation, the emphasis might be on the analysis of representatives as individual investment centres, i.e. by showing for each a separate sales and cost breakdown together with aspects of performance relating to such variables as:

- Calls made
- Orders obtained
- Average order size
- Discounts allowed
- Bad debts
- New customers and business obtained

For the sales office supporting this operation, the analysis might cover the costs of the different services provided and key measures of productivity, for example:

- The number of orders processed
- The proportion of deliveries made on time
- Returns by customers, resulting, for example, from errors in pricing, invoicing, product specification, delivery, etc.

Reflected in all of these measures of performance are the skills of those involved, both individually and collectively. In essence, they provide the key to 'objective training'. Shortfalls in performance or changes in performance standards therefore inevitably point to training needs.

This sort of analysis can be carried out for any function, not just those at the 'sharp end' or where measurement of performance has been traditional. Later in this chapter, examples are given of stock control and revenue accounting and Appendix 2 provides a basis for considering its application elsewhere.

Other elements of cost

Other useful insights into a company's performance can be gained by examining fixed and variable costs. For example, in examining the relationship between sales growth and pre-tax profits of a business, it might be observed that the company appears to have a particular problem in controlling its costs in line with output. Among other things, this may point to the need to examine the extent to which the company's cost structure makes it vulnerable to changes in sales volume. The information obtained would highlight training priorities.

Where this is the case, a vulnerability ratio can be calculated by dividing fixed costs by operating profits. This ratio reflects the extent to which a business may be operating near to its break-even point and its profits therefore vulnerable to relatively small changes in volume—the lower the ratio of fixed costs to operating profits, the less vulnerable the business is to a decline in sales volume. By the same token, it can also be used to reflect the potential for significant improvements in profits.

By breaking down these costs further (for example, into direct and indirect costs according to products and markets), it is possible to form a view on which activities are really generating satisfactory returns or otherwise. This is particularly valuable where resources are scarce. From a training perspective it can help in making certain decisions—for instance, whether and how much to invest in training effort and where to direct it (towards, for example, improving unsatisfactory performance or building upon evident strengths). In the process it can be seen that contribution analysis provides a very sound basis upon which to raise many questions about a company's sales and marketing policies and the associated skills and the level of training provision.

Financial performance ratios

Turnover of working capital

$$\frac{\text{Sales}}{\text{Working capital}}$$

Changes in the rate of turnover of working capital reflect the effectiveness of its use in generating sales and the skills of the organization in financial management. Generally, from a performance point of view, the faster it is turned over, the better—it implies efficiency in its use. However, if the turnover is too rapid, it can indicate that there is insufficient working capital in the business. The risk inherent in this is that, if sales were suddenly to fall, suppliers to harden their terms, or debtors to take extended credit, the company might be strapped for cash.

Current ratio

$$\frac{\text{Current assets}}{\text{Current liabilities}}$$

The current ratio provides a measure of the solvency of a business, i.e. its ability to pay its debts. Traditionally, companies with a current ratio of 2 or higher have been regarded as 'safe' and therefore in a sound position to borrow. In practice, many companies operate as a matter of policy on current ratios of 1.5 or even less.

A company which buys on credit but sells for cash may be in a particularly good position to operate on a low ratio. Conversely, one which sells on adverse terms compared with those on which it buys is likely to have to maintain a higher ratio.

The immediate cause of a business failing is usually that it has insufficient cash to meet its liabilities as they fall due. From everyone's point of view, including the trainer's, the important consideration is therefore the trend. Thus, if a business's current ratio is deteriorating below manageable levels there is almost certainly scope and need for the trainer to give priority attention to the effectiveness of training for those concerned.

Acid test/liquidity ratio

$$\frac{\text{Liquid assets}}{\text{Current liabilities}}$$

As its name implies, this is a more stringent ratio than the current ratio. It can be used to gauge the liquidity of a business, i.e. its ability to meet its current liabilities from 'liquid' assets. Liquid assets are those which can be realized relatively quickly, hence they include cash and debtors, but not stocks and work in progress.

The ratio is calculated by dividing cash and debtors by current liabilities. Generally, a ratio of 1 or greater is regarded as satisfactory, but different types of businesses will have different appropriate levels. Again, the important consideration is the trend.

Turnover of stocks

$$\frac{\text{Sales}}{\text{Stocks}}$$

Where stocks consist solely of bought-in items, this ratio can be thought of as the number of times per year in which the stock is sold and replaced, i.e. turned over. It can be helpful to present this on a days, weeks or months basis (by multiplying the reciprocal of the ratio by, for example, the number of days in the year).

For many businesses it is insufficient simply to divide sales by stocks and it is necessary to treat raw materials and work in progress separately, using different ratios. Thus raw materials are better related to materials consumed and work in progress to the value of production.

The aim of using the ratios is to assess whether stocks are higher than necessary, thereby tying up working capital and limiting the use of fixed assets, or too low, resulting in stock shortages which can cause production blockages and adversely affect sales. Additionally, the quickening rate of change and the generally shortened life-span of products point to the need for the business to improve constantly its rate of stock turnover to avoid being left with unsaleable stock.

It needs to be recognized also that where stocks are excessive, or form a high proportion of working capital, worsening market conditions may result in price falls, necessitating substantial write-offs against profits. An indicator of stock vulnerability can be calculated by dividing stocks by working capital.

These issues point to the need for trainers to keep a particularly close eye on:

- The amount of money tied up in stocks
- The incidence of stock shortages
- Levels of wastage and loss

Where these ratios reflect that all is not well, they can represent a special opportunity for trainers—a veritable gold mine—to review the effectiveness of procedures, work allocation and supervision, job design and the associated training provision, extending way beyond the stock-control function into the associated functions of purchasing, production control and sales.

However, these are 'specifics', and it is important at this stage not to lose sight of the need to stand back in order to form a more general view of management's performance and skills and the wider training implications—i.e. the extent to which problems in one part of a business may be symptomatic of problems elsewhere.

Turnover of debtors

$$\frac{\text{Sales}}{\text{Debtors}}$$

Assuming that all sales are on credit, the turnover of debtors ratio reveals the number of times per year that debtors are turned over. Where the business sells for cash as well as on credit, it makes sense to strip out cash sales. By using the reciprocal of the ratio multiplied by the number of days in the year, the ratio indicates the number of days' credit allowed to customers, thus permitting easy comparison with the organization's terms and conditions of payment. As with stocks, the name of the game is to avoid tying up working capital more than is necessary and thereby save financing costs. In addition, old debts are more likely to become bad debts.

There are very few businesses which could not improve their performance in this area. Indeed, recent research indicates that the late payment of commercial debts costs British companies the equivalent of more than half their net profits, or 5.7 per cent of annual turnover (Justitia Unicol, 1990).

Clearly, within this area of business, there are often tremendous training opportunities. These relate particularly to ensuring understanding of the purpose, priorities and applications of debt-control procedures and developing flexibility and responsiveness among staff who carry them out.

From the training standpoint the process also offers the attractive potential of yielding quick results for a relatively low level of investment. The results feed straight through into the profit and loss account (for example, in the form of reduced financing costs) and to an improved cash position in the balance sheet. Improved performance can readily be translated into a tangible benefit of training and all that is implied in terms of attitudes to training and the credibility of the trainer.

Creditor ratio   As an adjunct to the acid test and debtor ratios it can be instructive to calculate the credit ratio:

$$\frac{\text{Purchases}}{\text{Creditors}}$$

By comparing the ratio for credit taken against that for credit given, an indication of possible strains on liquidity in the future can be provided. Multiplying the reciprocal of the ratio by the number of days in the year expresses the ratio in terms of days taken to pay suppliers. It should also be noted that the ratio may suggest that a company is delaying payment to suppliers as a means of increasing the amount of available working capital and meeting financial liabilities as they fall due. In turn, whereas the dividing line between may be a fine one, it would be cause for concern to observe that a business was taking an inordinately long time to pay its bills.

Other financial performance ratios

A number of other financial ratios can be calculated—for example, those which may be used to assess the financial stability of the business and its potential as an investment. Particularly important among these is the gearing ratio.

Gearing/leverage ratio

$$\frac{\text{Fixed interest capital}}{\text{Shareholders' funds}}$$

The gearing ratio shows the rationship between fixed-interest capital and shareholders' funds. In consequence, it reflects the extent to which the business is financed by capital on which it has to pay fixed returns and which are paid with priority over dividends on equity. Such capital includes loans, mortgages, debentures and preference shares. The lower the gearing, the more likely the returns on equity capital to mirror changes in profits, because relatively little of its profits have to be paid as interest. In contrast, given that the business can generate returns in excess of borrowing rates, a certain level of borrowing can be highly beneficial to shareholders, since the surplus accrues to them.

As a general rule, a business with a gearing of less than 0.4 is regarded as safe. However, any increase over this level increases the risk of it being forced out of business by disaffected creditors.

Two further associated ratios are those for showing the extent of 'interest cover' and 'dividend cover'. The lower the cover, the more likely it is that declining profits, and hence cash generation, will threaten the ability to make dividend and interest payments.

Return on shareholders' capital

One criterion for success in running a business is likely to be the net returns to shareholders. Accordingly, obtaining growth in earnings in excess of the rate of inflation may be a key objective for management to achieve. This can be expressed either as a measure of profitability of shareholders' capital (i.e. net profit after tax divided by net worth) or earnings per share.

Conclusion

In conclusion, it can be seen that ratio analysis can be an extremely powerful tool for assessing the performance of a business and hence areas of training opportunity, need and priority. In doing so, however, the caveats relating to the reliability and use of accounting information need to be borne in mind. Appendix 1 concludes with a summary of these.

More important still, the interpretation of ratios requires skill and discretion, i.e. training and practice, particularly when seeking to form perceptions and draw conclusions about 'soft' and underlying meanings from 'hard' numerical data. Ratio analysis is therefore best regarded as a starting point for further investigation and as part of the overall process of assessing training needs and developing a training strategy—but a starting point which gives the trainer an unusual opportunity to really relate to the needs of the business.[1]

Note

1 The suggestions for further reading given in the previous chapter are equally relevant here.

Reference

Justitia Unicol, (1990), *Getting Paid*, Harrow, Middx.

Conclusion to Part Three

Financial appraisal is central to the Training for Profit approach. This is because, as a tool of analysis, it provides a means of assessing and reflecting the performance, strengths, weaknesses and potential of almost every part and function of an organization.

For most organizations the starting point for financial analysis is the ratio of the return on capital employed or return on assets, since these represent fundamental indicators of profitability and reflect the extent to which an organization generates returns proportionate to the resources invested. As the analysis progresses the ratios build up systematically into an integrated set that can be used to quantify, examine and explain the contribution which the various parts of an organization make towards overall success. This provides the basis upon which to assess the implications of the information revealed and the associated training needs. Some questions to consider are:

What are the key financial measures of success of your organization? How do these translate into ratios for:
—Overall management performance?
—Operating performance?
—Main elements of cost?
—Financial performance?

In using them, what *caveats* relating to the reliability and use of accounting information need to be borne in mind? If you feel unsure of your skills in this area, who could you turn to for advice?

PART FOUR

The role and skills of the trainer

Introduction

The purpose of the preceding chapters has been to put across the conceptual foundations of the Training for Profit approach and to provide a set of tools for carrying out an overall assessment of training needs. However, as emphasized in Chapter 2, it is the actual process of carrying out the assessment of strengths and weaknesses of the organization and their translation into skills that is the key to success. For it is by undertaking this process that the trainer really has the opportunity to reflect where, why, how and when training can help to improve and develop the performance and effectiveness of the organization in both the short and long terms.

For the process to be effective the trainer requires two things:

1 A framework for action
2 Skills in managing the process

The next two chapters therefore aim to provide a focus on factors to be taken into account in establishing a framework for action, and reviews the role and skills of the trainer in managing the process of conducting the assessment of training needs and planning how best to meet them.

8 Getting on with it— a framework for action

For a problem-solving approach like Training for Profit to be successful, it needs to be carried out as objectively as possible and to reflect the views of everyone likely to be affected by the process or its outcomes. It is essential, therefore, that the responsibility for assessing overall training and staff development needs lies with a senior manager—ideally, the chief executive—in order to reflect its importance and significance and the organization's commitment to training its workforce.

Appointing the assessor

Whoever is given the job of actually carrying out the work should be in a position to report directly to the Board. In a large organization, the process of assessing training needs is going to be a complex one. The assessment is therefore likely to be carried out most effectively by a training specialist or a consultant specializing in this field in close consultation with the managers and staff involved.

In a medium-sized organization the best results are likely to be achieved by whichever senior manager has overall responsibility for staff development and training, drawing upon specialist help from within and outside the organization as and when required. In a small organization it would be appropriate for the assessment to be carried out by the chief executive acting in consultation with the entire management team and all those concerned. It would also be highly appropriate to draw upon the services of a training specialist, not just to facilitate the task but also to gain an outsider's perspective.

The importance of process

So far, it can be seen that reviewing the organization's objectives, strategy and performance in financial terms highlights the direction of long-term training and staff-development strategy as well as establishing the scope for assessing priorities for potential training contributions in the shorter term. It is at this point that trainers need to bring into play their 'process' skills in order to secure agreement and commitment to training plans and their implementation. Up to this point the process is likely to have centred primarily on the gathering and analysis of information—both hard and soft—to give them an understanding of the business. This in itself provides trainers with an important tool—for it is through the process of presenting it that the opportunity for changing attitudes, and ultimately behaviour, can be found. A more detailed discussion of how this can be done is given in Chapter 9.

Assessing training needs involves discussions with managers and key personnel at appropriate points and levels of the organization. The main purpose of these discussions is to check out their perceptions on the nature and overall performance of the organization, the contribution their particular function makes to its effectiveness and to start to identify any related training needs.

It can be useful to consider four stages within these discussions:

1 Analysis of the organization's performance and plans
2 Examination of strengths and weaknesses
3 Assessment of implications for developing skills
4 Translation into training priorities and plans.

To get the most out of these discussions, the trainer needs to work at two distinct levels of analysis. At one level, he or she gathers information and compares it with 'standards' and 'values' which allow an assessment of the effectiveness of whatever aspect of the business is under consideration. At another, underlying, level the trainer needs to be able to focus attention on and reflect the extent to which managers and key personnel:

- Appear to be abreast of current and likely future developments in their field
- Are aware of what it is they are trying to achieve and, more specifically, whether they have a plan outlining how they will get there
- Have the necessary resources to achieve their plans
- Have organized and trained their staff in a way that is likely to achieve the objectives, now and in the future
- Have effective mechanisms to assess progress towards achieving their plans and objectives (e.g. control and performance review systems)
- Are aware of their performance
- Are able to take remedial action where necessary
- Understand the relationship between their function and the rest of the business

To some trainers and managers, certain of these aspects may seem presumptuous—particularly if their experience of training has been limited to, or constrained by, traditional methods. However, with the Training for Profit approach there is an underlying assumption that those with responsibility for training have not only an exceptional opportunity but also an obligation to participate in the assessment of the quality of their organization's workforce. Only by doing so will they be able to develop coherent training policies and plans to ensure increasing effectiveness and credible solutions to their organization's need for skills.

Scope of the discussion

The main subjects for discussion are those which reflect the strategy and performance of the organization as a whole as well as its principal operating functions. Thus, from an overall perspective the review process is likely to cover the following:

1 Broad description of the organization
2 Context of the organization, i.e. its environment
3 Overall objectives, policies, strategies and plans
4 Functional operations, for example:
   —Marketing
   —Sales
   —Distribution
   —Research and development
   —Production and service
   —Finance
   —Purchasing
   —Stocks and materials
   —Personnel and training
5 Organization structure and culture

Within this framework it can be seen that the trainer's awareness of the organization, its performance and context is vital, as is his or her conceptual ability to understand and classify forms of organization and organizational behaviour. Additionally, he or she needs to possess appropriate intervention skills as well as the capacity to raise questions which get to the heart of the matter. Indeed, it is these abilities and skills which make the difference between a mechanistic and a developmental approach.

Examples of the questions which might be relevant in particular situations are given in Appendix 2. However, this is not intended to be used as a comprehensive checklist, but as an *aide-mémoire* to help structure and review the progress of the survey. It can therefore be adapted to the issues and priorities indicated by the findings of the review of the organization's strategy and performance.

Assessing the needs

The review of the organization's strategy and performance is likely to highlight the existence of training needs and opportunties at four levels:

1 Organizational
2 Functional
3 Occupational
4 Individual

It is also probable that skills will need to be developed to ensure that the organization has the capacity to relate effectively to its environment. Thus at one level all organizations have to adapt to their environment and change within it. At another level, organizations—even small ones—have the potential opportunity to influence their environments. They do this by, for example, tackling new markets, developing new products, adopting new technologies, or introducing new employment and training policies.

The next step is to assess the underlying strengths and weaknesses of the organization in terms of the skills it possesses and identify those areas in which skills need to be developed. This process, besides supporting and encouraging a broader approach to training among managers at every level, should also result in the identification of specific opportunities to achieve more effective use of people by:

- Removing barriers to effectiveness
- Allocating training resources to priority needs
- Creating learning opportunities for individual and team development
- Reducing role conflict, particularly at organizational boundaries
- Providing an increased sense of identity

Preparing the plan

On completion of this stage the trainer should have reached agreement on the major training priorities within the business. This should include their respective potential contributions to improved performance and future plans in measurable terms—e.g. profits—and the time scale for their achievement. In the process, the trainer will also have had the opportunity to establish and enhance credibility and the capacity of the training function to help. This can be accomplished by:

1 Formulating action areas as a basis for planning the training
2 Establishing priorities
3 Identifying those involved and needing to be trained
4 Defining the nature of training required in terms of the changes required in attitudes, knowledge and skills and the standards of performance to be achieved
5 Determining the methods of training to be adopted
6 Allocating and agreeing responsibility for carrying out the training
7 Setting target dates for the start and completion of training
8 Specifying expected costs and benefits
9 Agreeing the procedure for reviewing and controlling training and progress towards achieving the identified action areas

Management of training

In essence, the management of training is synonymous with the management of change. Milan Kubr (1986) puts this nicely in his review of consulting and change in his assertion that:

The human dimension of organizational change is a fundamental one. For it is people in the organization—its managerial and technical staff and other workers—whose behaviour ultimately determines what organizational changes can be made and what real benefits can be drawn from them. It is so because organizations are human systems above all. People must understand, and be willing and able to implement, changes which at first glance may appear purely technological and structural, but will in fact affect people in some way.

In coping with organizational change, people have to change too: they must acquire new knowledge, absorb more information, tackle new tasks, upgrade their skills, and, very often, modify their work habits, values and attitudes to the way of doing things in the organization. Change in values and attitudes is essential. There probably cannot be any real change without a change in attitude (p.55).

This raises two basic issues for the trainer. First, where does the responsibility for training lie? Second, what is the appropriate framework for implementing the training plan?

The first question is more easily answered than the second, since the responsibility for training should lie with senior management. It is only senior management who have the authority and means to promote understanding of its purpose throughout the organization and ensure the cooperation of those involved. This, in turn, highlights the importance of their support for the entire assessment process and its function in providing a sound basis for the overall planning of training needs.

Although this may seem to beg the question of persuasion at this level, in practice the task is generally less daunting than it might seem. This is because the inherent characteristic of the Training for Profit approach of assessing training contributions in financial terms makes it relatively easy for management to 'buy' a well-argued proposition. After all, most managers are under extreme pressure to improve the cost effectiveness or profitability of their operation.

Deciding upon a framework for implementing the training plan is less easy, since it is dependent not only upon the identification of training needs but also upon:

- The organization's attitude and openness to training
- The amount of training that can be accommodated
- The level of commitment from those involved
- The nature and kind of training that is acceptable
- The skills of the trainer in gaining support

This is particularly the case where training in the past has been poorly planned, organized and managed.

Approaches using project teams

However, experience has suggested that one particularly effective approach involves using project teams. Their relevance and usefulness to organizational effectiveness, described by Professor Bernard Taylor in *The Management Development and Training Handbook* (1984) is just as great to those using the Training for Profit approach:

The project team approach has the advantage in cutting through the usual lines of authority and responsibility and releasing ideas and energy at lower levels in the organization. It is a particularly good way of galvanizing a company into action to cope with a crisis, resulting, e.g., from a fall in sales, the appearance of a new competitor, or a switch-over to a new technology. From a management development point of view, project teams allow staff at all levels to exercise initiatives and to gain an understanding of areas of business in which they are not normally involved (p.21).

A typical approach can be in four stages:

1 Those with overall responsibility for training specify the action required and formulate broad objectives, criteria and constraints for their accomplishment.
2 Projects are allocated to staff drawn appropriately from across the organization.
3 Project leaders, generally senior managers, are appointed.
4 Dates are set for reporting back and reviewing progress and results achieved.

It is important to remember that training will need to be provided which is relevant to both the project and the requirements of those involved. Besides the organization's own training resources, this may require the use of external agencies (for example, consultants and colleges).

References

Kubr, M. (ed.) (1986) *Management Consulting—A Guide to the Profession*, 2nd edition, Geneva: ILO.

Taylor, B. (1984) 'Management training and development in the 1980's', in B. Taylor and G. Lippitt (eds) *The Management Development and Training Handbook*, 2nd edition, Maidenhead: McGraw-Hill.

9 Getting results—the skills of the trainer

The trainer's role

Training for Profit is concerned with organizational change. However, in bringing about change, the trainer will rarely be responsible for managing the change process itself, since this is primarily the function of line management. Thus the role of the trainer is generally that of facilitating. A perhaps unusual, but valuable, example of this is provided by the managing director of a small confectionery business.

The overall assessment of training needs had been carried out and the main recommendations presented to the company's senior management. They accepted the principal suggestions without hesitation—not least because they provided clarification of their own concerns and a forum in which to do so. So far, so good! But when it came to implementation, there was a clear reluctance to act. This was not inconsistent with the need identified for skills in decision making during the assessment process. It was therefore agreed that an appropriate way to meet these needs would be to set up a series of short meetings with the managing director. Their purpose would be to review progress periodically and regularly—i.e. the decisions he had made.

After some weeks of what seemed to be no progress whatsoever, our meetings had become characterized by long silences and were becoming a little awkward, to say the least. Indeed, they reached the point when, one day, I put it to him that I really didn't think I could justify coming to see him for much longer, and that I felt bad about taking his money for what appeared to be nothing in return. His reply, which came after an uncharacteristic short pause, took my breath away, for what it taught me about the management of 'process', in general, and decision making in particular.

Through our meetings, he said, he had come to see that his inaction was as much a decision as action. Shifting from one state to another therefore raised very deep personal issues. However frustrating and unsatisfactory these meetings might be from my point of view, he continued, they were most important to him. Given time, he felt, they would result in action. And so they did, but that's another story . . .

Essential skills

In the main, however, the trainer's role is more akin to that of a consultant.

This means that the trainer needs to possess relevant skills in facilitating change. These can be classified under the broad headings of:

- Technical skills
- People skills
- Intervention/influencing skills.

From the *technical* perspective, the trainer needs to possess the skills to identify, assess, plan and meet the training opportunities and needs across their organization. This includes problem-solving skills, i.e. identifying problems, gathering and analysing relevant information and choosing between alternative courses of action. They also need to be familiar with, and be able to apply, the knowledge and skills traditionally associated with the trainer's role, e.g. learning theory, training design, instructional techniques and so on.

In addition to these, a much broader understanding of people at work is also required. The sort of *people* skills needed include an appreciation of human development, motivation, role theory, group processes, and alternative styles of management as well as sources of power and influence.

Trainers also need a broad understanding of organizations and their contexts, including, for example, an awareness of the environment, the major functions of organizations, fundamental planning and control systems, and alternative ways of organizing work and structuring organizations. Even more importantly, they need to be able to appreciate the interaction of these diverse aspects of organizations and assess their potential and actual effect on performance.

The *intervention* skills required by the trainer are primarily those associated with the process of establishing, managing and developing relationships at different levels within the organization, together with a keen awareness of the ways in which people react to change and can be helped to bring it about.

Managing the assessment process

Training for Profit entails systematic and disciplined work and the search for creative and effective solutions. Essentially there are five phases in the process of carrying out the assessment:

1 Planning
 —Formulating the main stages of the assessment
 —Identifying preliminary contacts
 —Obtaining access to information
 —Setting target dates for completion
 —Gaining consent and cooperation from key people, e.g. managers, supervisors, personnel and training staff and employee representatives
 —Establishing criteria for success
2 Diagnosis
 —Data gathering
 —Data analysis

—Specific problem analysis
3 Evaluation
   —Assessing priorities
   —Identifying possible solutions
   —Evaluating alternatives
   —Formulating proposals
4 Action planning
   —Presenting findings
   —Discussing possible solutions
   —Agreeing courses of action
   —Preparing action plans
5 Implementation
   —Providing support and assistance
   —Responding to changing situations
   —Assessing validity
   —Reviewing effectiveness

In the *planning* phase the principal objective needs to be to tune the organization into what is going to follow and to gain commitment to it. Time spent planning is rarely wasted and the success of the survey will largely depend on how well the groundwork has been done. It is therefore essential that the trainer has a clear idea of what is to be attempted and the capacity to focus on developing constructive relationships with the individuals identified as significant to the success of the survey.

The *diagnosis* stage is primarily concerned with data gathering and analysis. This requires examination of information from inside and outside the organization and consideration of any improvements that might be made in working practices. It is during this stage that financial ratio analysis really comes into its own.

Most of the time involved in this stage is likely to be spent in discussion and interviews with managers, supervisors and other employees in order to consider performance and identify the nature and extent of changes required. The quality of the diagnosis is crucial, since it serves as the basis upon which subsequent decisions will be made. It is also an integral part of the change process and can of itself be expected to affect attitudes and, consequently, behaviour, decisions and performance.

The *evaluation* phase needs to result in the establishment of priorities and consideration of alternative solutions and courses of action. It is at this point that trainers really need to bring into play the technical skills at their disposal as an effective means of solving problems of human performance. Besides demanding careful attention to detail and the adoption of a systematic approach to reviewing alternatives, it calls for imagination and creativity to find solutions which are relevant, feasible and appealing to those involved.

Action planning is concerned with gaining acceptance of the need for change and reaching agreement on how it can be brought about. It is therefore particularly important to attempt to anticipate potential areas of resistance to change and to consider ways in which it might be overcome.

It is one thing to reach agreement on the content of a training plan, quite another to ensure its *implementation*. This stage is concerned with providing support and assistance directed towards fulfilling the objectives of the plan. It is therefore important not only to be flexible and responsive to changing situations but also to accept that the training plan may need to be modified as a result of either faulty analysis at an earlier stage or changes in the situation of the organization. Thus the plan needs to be kept under continuous review, to ensure not only that the training to be provided is relevant but also that the effectiveness of the approach can be developed.

Influencing change

As mentioned at the beginning of this chapter, the process of bringing about change is likely to require changes in patterns of behaviour and, even more fundamentally, the development of new attitudes and values. For the trainer this raises two central issues.

The first concerns understanding the change process and, in particular, developing a keen awareness of the sort of conditions which result in resistance to change. The second relates to the processes of bringing about change and what this means for the approach and strategy to be adopted by the trainer.

Different people change in different ways and every person is unique in terms of their willingness and ability to adapt to change. Even so, it is not surprising that resistance to change is likely where those affected will be left worse off than they were before (for example, in terms of their job, position in the organization, pay and conditions of work and so on).

However, a great deal of resistance may also be met if the proposed change is neutral, or even beneficial to the persons concerned. This observation was made by Milan Kubr (1986). He suggests that resistance will stem from:

—Lack of conviction that change is needed. If people are not properly informed and the purpose of change is not explained to them, they are likely to view the present situation as satisfactory and an effort to change as useless and upsetting.

—Dislike of imposed change. In general, people do not like to be treated as passive objectives. They resent changes that are imposed on them and about which they cannot express any views.

—Dislike of surprises. People do not want to be kept in the dark about any change that is being prepared; managerial decisions bringing about important changes tend to be resented if they come as a surprise.

—Fear of the unknown. Basically, people do not like to live in uncertainty and may prefer an imperfect present to an unknown and uncertain future.

—Reluctance to deal with unpopular issues. Managers and other people often try to avoid unpleasant reality and unpopular actions, even if they realize that they will not be able to avoid these for ever.

—Fear of inadequacy and failure. Many people worry about their ability to adjust to change and maintain and improve their performance in a new work situation. Some of them may feel insecure and doubt their ability to make a special effort to learn new skills.

—Disturbed practices, habits and relations. Following organizational change, well established and fully-mastered practices and work habits may become obsolete, and familiar relationships may be altered or totally destroyed. This can lead to considerable frustration and unhappiness.

—Lack of respect and trust in the person promoting change. People are suspicious about change proposed by a manager whom they do not trust and respect, or by an external person whose competence and motives are not known and understood (p.58).

Although some of these causes of resistance to change may be regarded as human nature, they tend to be reinforced through experience. This is particularly the case where change in the past has been experienced as harmful.

Models for change

In planning for change it can be helpful to consider the application of Kurt Lewin's (1951) approach using force-field analysis. Conceptually, the underlying theory regards any behaviour as being the result of an equilibrium between 'driving' and 'restraining forces'—see Figure 9.1.

The implication of the theory is that any change of behaviour is a result of disequilibrium, which can be created by changing either driving or restraining forces (for example, by increasing or decreasing existing forces, or by adding new ones). In applying the approach it is worth bearing in mind that, in general, multiple causes of behaviour need to be considered rather than single ones. Moreover, reducing resisting forces will often be more effective than increasing driving forces—hence the power of such questions as 'What stops you doing a better job?'

Another helpful model for understanding, planning and influencing change is the learning curve and its components—see Figure 9.2. When applying the model, it is important to understand that the stages of a learning curve are sequential and that trainers omit stages at their peril. The objective, therefore, is to minimize the duration of each stage, thereby increasing the slope of the curve.

The learning curve model is consistent with Lewin's change model, which is based upon three sequential stages of *unfreezing*, *changing* and *refreezing*. The unfreezing stage is primarily concerned with creating awareness of the risks and likely outcomes if the organization does not change.

Changing consists of two phases: *identification* and *internalization*. Identification involves making provision for those affected to test out the proposed changes. Internalization is concerned with structuring learning to transform the proposals for change into personal goals and behaviour.

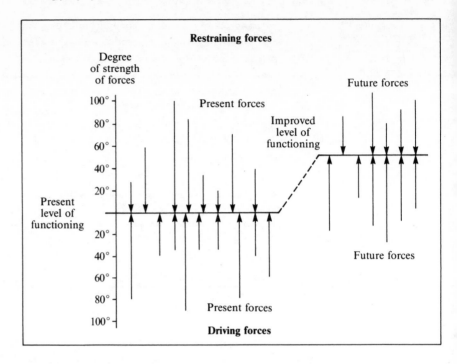

Figure 9.1 *Force-field analysis*
(Source: Kubr, 1986: reproduced with permission of the publisher)

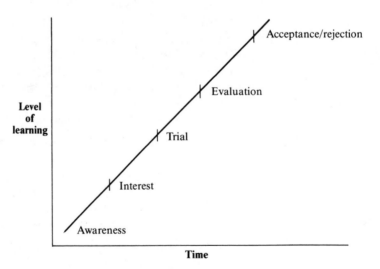

Figure 9.2 *Change as a learning process*

Refreezing is the process of verifying the change through experience. It can be assisted by the appropriate provision of a supportive environment, psychological and material rewards and positive reinforcement. This model is brought vividly to life in Bill Reddin's (1988) description of the fish tank experiment, in which a large fish is separated from small ones by a glass partition, so that it can see them but cannot get at them. In the process, however bizarre the analogy, he mirrors precisely what so often happens in organizations, large and small. What happens, quite routinely, is that:

the big fish attempts to get closer to the small fish but continually bumps into the partition. After doing this a few hundred times, the fish gets rather sore and stops doing it. So far what has happened is rather obvious; what happens next is not. The glass partition is removed, the small fish surround the big fish and the big fish makes no attempt to eat them. The big fish in fact dies in a sea of plenty. It has learned only too well that the small fish are unavailable, and that if you try to reach them, pain will result. It has great difficulty in unlearning what it has already learned so well. The fish has been conditioned to be unable to learn or respond to a new situation (pp. 101–2).

As Reddin concludes, this experiment reflects what may be routinely observed in planned change programmes. Thus:

management thinks it is a good idea to 'remove the glass'—this may be their wish to introduce a new climate or new methods in the organization. Other managers in the organization (most having been around for a long time with a different system) have learned only too well not to 'go after the smaller fish'. Top management may initiate training courses, wave flags or give speeches concerning the fact that they have removed the glass, but middle managers simply do not believe it and do not respond. Their problem is that they have some unlearning to do because their prior learning was so good! In short, they need 'unfreezing'. They need to be able to see the reality of their current changed situation rather than what used to be there.

These approaches can be seen to rest upon the assumption that change takes place at various levels and is primarily dependent upon achieving behavioural change through changes in knowledge and attitudes. As such, they tend to exclude the opposite position whereby behaviour influences attitudes and knowledge.

This situation is captured nicely in change strategies which contrast participative and coercive approaches. For example, Paul Hersey and Kenneth Blanchard's model (1972), shown in Figure 9.3, not only reflects the relationship between change in individuals, people and organizations but also suggests the time span and level of difficulty involved for various levels of change.

It can be seen that the participative approach commences with knowledge changes, leading through changes in attitudes and individual behaviour to organizational or group behaviour change. In contrast, the coercive approach relies on bringing pressure to bear on organizational or group behaviour. Most trainers, in most situations, are likely to have to rely on participative approaches. However, they are generally reck-

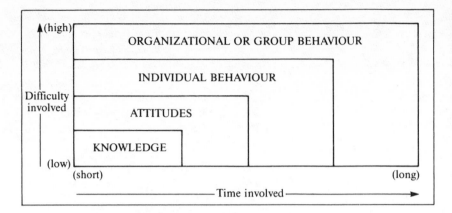

Figure 9.3   *Time span and level of difficulty involved for various levels of change*
(Source: Hersey and Blanchard, 1972)

oned to require a relatively mature and independent target population, since the goals set depend upon the workforce being motivated by a sense of personal achievement for their accomplishment. It is also important that the person initiating the change has sufficient credibility to influence the group.

On the other hand, the coercive approach can be seen to be inherently transient, since it is externally imposed and reliant upon the exercise of positional, rather than personal, power. Hence, the removal of the power source may result in a return to previous behaviour. It is also dependent upon the use of sanctions and rewards.

It may be, therefore, that the coercive approach is best used with groups and organizations whose members have a tendency towards, or history of, dependency and where quick results need to be obtained. In contrast, the participative approach, though possibly relatively slow and evolutionary, can generally be expected to achieve more durable change.

The trainer as a consultant

As has already been said, the trainer's role is very close to that of a consultant, who acts as both a resource and a facilitator of the process. As a resource, the trainer is responsible for the methodology and application of the approach to assessing training needs. This involves problem diagnosis, consideration of solutions and analysis of the training implications. In turn, it requires gaining the support of management in providing information, discussing progress and assessing proposals.

In terms of process, the trainer's aim is to help the organization to solve its own problems. The ways in which this is accomplished include creating awareness of organizational processes and their implications and consequences. The trainer should also be concerned with passing on and developing the skills of managing 'process' as opposed to 'task' so that the organization can learn to diagnose its own problems and develop its own solutions.

Thus, in using the Training for Profit approach, management collaboration and involvement is of the essence. As a result, the trainer's model is close to that of the set adviser in Action Learning. (For a full discussion of this, see Chapter 45 in Revans, 1982.) In order to carry out this role effectively, the trainer must possess the analytical and technical skills to reflect functional competence, while at the same time being credible in the role of observing problem-solving processes, providing feedback and raising questions for reflection.

References

Hersey, P. and K.H. Blanchard (1972) *Management of Organizational Behaviour*, Englewood Cliffs, NJ: Prentice Hall.

Kubr, M. (ed.) (1986) *Management Consulting—A Guide to the Profession*, 2nd edition, Geneva: ILO.

Lewin, K. (1951) *Field Theory in Social Science*, New York: Harper.

Reddin, W. (1988) *The Output-Oriented Organization*, Aldershot: Gower.

Revans, R.W. (1982) *The Origins and Growth of Action Learning*, London: Chartwell-Bratt.

Conclusion to Part Four

Whereas reviewing an organization's objectives, strategy and financial performance provides the basis for assessing training needs and priorities, it is the trainer's 'process' skills which are essential to securing agreement and commitment to training plans and their implementation. This involves discussions with managers and key personnel at appropriate points and levels of the organization in order to examine more closely:

- The underlying strengths and weaknesses of the organization
- The skills it possesses
- The areas in which skills need to be developed.

To carry out this process the trainer needs a sound understanding of organizational behaviour as a basis for intervention and raising questions which get to the heart of the matter. This is also central to the trainer's role in facilitating organizational change. Questions for consideration might include:

How comfortable do you feel about managing the assessment process and raising the sorts of questions and issues shown in Appendix 2?
What do attitudes towards training in your organization imply for formulating an intervention strategy?
What particular knowledge and skills do you need to be effective in this context?
To what extent are they possessed and how could they be developed?

PART FIVE

ABCO: A case study

Introduction

The purpose of the next three chapters is to provide an example of the Training for Profit approach in action. It focuses on ABCO, a business engaged in food preparation and wholesaling activities and illustrates:

1 The financial analysis applied to its year-end accounts and other data
2 The findings from the organization review in the context of its strategy, structure and culture
3 The action resulting, including the development of training strategies and plans to strike an appropriate balance between the achievement of improvements in performance in the short term and the longer-term development of organizational effectiveness
4 Examples and extracts from training design and implementation to show its connection and coherence with the company's strategy, structure and culture
5 A summary and discussion of the results achieved
6 The role and potential scope of the trainer

ABCO is a real company—only its name is fictional. With a turnover in the region of £2.5 million per annum many readers may regard it as small by comparison with their own organizations. However, its need for an additional £100 000 profits per annum does allow a useful perspective to be formed on the potential of training to contribute to business performance.

It should also be remembered that the principles underlying the approach are relevant to any organization, whatever its size—although, inevitably, with increasing size comes increasing complexity, in turn emphasizing the need for a conceptually sound, structured and systematic approach.

In presenting the financial analysis in the way shown it is also intended to provide a framework for practitioners new to the game to adopt for their own use. With a bit of ingenuity the principles can be applied to any organization. Indeed, examples include a ballet school and a convent.

At the other end of the spectrum, directors of quite large companies, feeling that they ought to know more about the business of training, have readily followed the various steps. The questions they were subsequently able to put to their training managers really were very testing indeed!

Some may be concerned that this appears a long and laborious approach. However, this need not be so. At ABCO, for example, despite a general lack of readily available information, carrying out the activities of financial analysis, organization review and report preparation took less than a week. Even in large organizations it is generally a question of weeks rather than months. Nor is it always necessary to carry out such a detailed financial review—management should already have the information and may be acting upon it, though not for training purposes. More than this, it needs to be remembered that carrying out the survey is as much a part of the process of developing and fostering attitudes to training as it is a means of assessing training needs.

10 Financial analysis

Introduction

The aim of this chapter is to provide a focus on the use and value of financial analysis as a tool to enable the trainer to get to grips with the business. The various tables in the text have been supplemented by graphs and other pictorial representations of some of the key figures they contain.

Background

ABCO is a member of a group of privately owned companies with interests ranging from property development to wholesaling and marketing. Each operating company is under the direction and control of the group managing director, who had been appointed some three years earlier in order to provide 'new blood' and ensure succession following the impending retirement of the company's two most senior directors.

During his period of office, the managing director had shown a particular concern to develop the company's property interests. One consequence of this had been the emergence of an overriding company policy of financial control and cash management, geared towards minimizing the external financing needs of these activities.

ABCO itself had been built up over many years by purveying best-quality fresh produce and service to the hotel, restaurant and catering trades. More recently, in tune with the needs of its customers, it has extended its product range by the addition of prepared, frozen and dry produce.

In recent years, despite relatively buoyant conditions reflected in the increased consumer awareness of the value of fruit and vegetables as part of a healthy and balanced diet, increasing competition and changes in the structure of the market had made trading difficult. In consequence, ABCO's sales revenues and profits had failed to make significant progress in real terms.

At an early stage the managing director responded to the company's deteriorating trading position and the difficult market conditions by developing the organizational structure and appointing additional managers in the areas of sales, production and finance. In consequence, the organization had attempted to move with considerable haste to a position of increased specialization and systematization. However, despite these developments, the problems and difficulties of profitably exploiting their policies and skills evidently persisted.

From the managing director's perspective, the performance of the business had reached a state where priority needed to be given to a vigorous attack on costs. This was reflected in his concern to find what he called his 'missing 4 per cent'—a reference to the deterioration in sales margins.

To some extent, this perception was shared by the sales and marketing director, in whose view most of the company's problems lay with the production and warehousing functions. This view was not, however, shared by the accountant, who felt, albeit hesitatingly, that the main need was for greater sales volume.

Financial structure and results

Balance sheet

An examination of ABCO's most recent balance sheet (Table 10.1) shows capital employed (shareholders' funds) of £518 237. This is being

Table 10.1 *Balance sheet of ABCO Ltd as at 31 December for the year t−1*

	£
Fixed assets	
Land and buildings	234 243
Machinery and plant	17 443
Fixtures and fittings	9 371
Vehicles	48 326
	309 383
Current assets	
Stocks	26 944
Debtors	386 862
Cash at bank and in hand	25 626
	439 432
Current liabilities	
Trade creditors	73 170
Overdraft	136 736
Other creditors	20 672
	230 578
Net current assets	208 854
Total assets less current liabilities	518 237
Creditors—amounts falling due after one year	—
Net assets	518 237
Capital and reserves	
Ordinary shares	1 350
Retained earnings	516 887
Shareholders' funds	518 237

used to finance fixed assets of £309 383 and net current assets (working capital) of £208 854.

In that current assets of £439 432 substantially exceed current liabilities, the company does not appear to have working capital problems. Moreover, since the company has no long-term external liabilities and owns land and buildings worth substantially more than that shown in the books, it appears to have considerable borrowing potential should the need arise.

Profit and loss account

The profit and loss account (Table 10.2) shows sales of over £2.6 million for the year, representing the total value of goods and services provided to customers. Any sales tax, such as VAT, has been deducted and so

Table 10.2 *Profit and loss account of ABCO Ltd for the year ended 31 December t−1*

	£	£
Sales		2 600 879
Opening stock	31 921	
Purchases	1 786 178	
Closing stock	(26 944)	
Cost of materials		1 791 155
Value added		809 724
Total wages		341 879
Sales expenses		
Commissions	126 948	
Travelling expenses	5 029	
Advertising	11 669	
Promotional	25 196	
Total sales expenses		168 842
Distribution expenses		66 148
Administration expenses		
Rent and rates	22 886	
Heat and light	12 280	
Communications	21 150	
Legal and professional	8 320	
Other	14 983	
Total administration expenses		79 619
Directors' emoluments		71 300
Maintenance expenses		13 671
Depreciation		29 809
Total wages and expenses		771 268
Operating profit		38 456
Interest expense		16 327
Profit on ordinary activities before tax		22 129

Note.   In this table taxes and net profit after tax have not been shown, nor have expenses for research and development.

have returned goods. Deducting the cost of materials results in an added value figure of just under £810 000.

Wages and other expenses amount to £771 268, resulting in operating profits of £38 456. After deducting interest paid (less any receivable) ABCO earned pre-tax profits of £22 129. Given sales of just over £2.6 million, this doesn't seem very much.

Statement of source and application of funds

The funds flow statement for ABCO (Table 10.3) shows that internally generated cash amounted to £52 000, resulting largely from the provision for depreciation rather than profits. Some 80 per cent of these internally generated funds were used to meet liabilities for tax and the balance on the purchase of new assets. No dividend has been paid.

Table 10.3 *Statement of sources and application of funds of ABCO Ltd for the year ended 31 December t−1*

Sources of funds	
Pre-tax profit	22 000
Depreciation	30 000
Total generated from operations	52 000
Funds from other sources	Nil
	52 000
Application of funds	
Purchases of fixed assets	12 000
Taxation	43 000
Dividends paid	Nil
	55 000
Net outflow of funds	(3 000)
Increase/(decrease) in working capital	
Decrease in stocks	(5 000)
Decrease in debtors	(18 000)
Decrease in creditors, excluding corporation tax	3 000
	(20 000)
Changes in net liquid funds	
Increase in cash at bank and in hand	2 000
Decrease in borrowing	15 000
Net decrease in working capital	(3 000)

The statement also shows a reduction in working capital of £20 000, largely as a result of a reduction in debtors. This has allowed a modest reduction in borrowing.

What the statements mean

This preliminary examination of ABCO's financial results suggests that the company is finding progress difficult. There appear to be insufficient internally generated funds to provide adequately for the development and expansion of the business.

The movements in working capital are relatively small, but perhaps reflect an attempt to improve financial control within the business. At the same time, the business is not short of capital and has considerable underlying strength in that it has no long-term external liabilities.

From a training perspective, the implication is that there is a need to focus on identifying more closely the underlying causes of the company's shortfall in trading performance, reflected by the lack of stated profits. In turn, this implies a careful analysis not just of levels of profitability but also of the trend over a period of years. Additionally, this provides the context for raising a number of important and fundamental questions such as:

- What is happening to sales?
- What is happening to productivity?
- How are costs controlled?

Only by doing so will it be possible to develop relevant training strategies directed towards improving profitability and cash flow generation.

ABCO's underlying financial strength suggests that the company is not yet in serious difficulties. However, the level of funds generated from operations is far from satisfactory. Its general financial position does not suggest that money for investing in training will be easy to come by. This means that training expenditure will need to be carefully justified not just to obtain the approval of management but also so as not exacerbate the company's problems.

This highlights the need to direct training investment specifically towards efforts to improve the company's operating performance. In the process, it will be crucial to strike the appropriate balance between short-, medium- and long-term needs. The next step is to conduct a more detailed financial analysis using the techniques of ratio analysis.

Financial ratio analysis

Overall performance ratios

Table 10.4 shows ABCO's overall management performance figures. (See also Figs. 10.1, 10.2 and 10.3). During the period it can be seen that sales have shown little progress in real terms and pre-tax profits appear to have declined significantly since the period *t*-2. If allowances are made for inflation, the amount of capital employed is actually declining steadily in real terms.

Table 10.4 *Overall performance ratios*

| | Year | | | |
	−3	−2	−1	Current (9 months)
Sales (£000's)	2240	2466	2601	1933
Pre-tax profit (PTP)	38	56	22	7
Capital employed	487	507	518	526
% PTP to capital	7.8	11.0	4.2	2.0*
% PTP to sales	1.7	2.3	0.8	0.4*
Turnover of capital	4.6	4.9	5.0	5.0*

*Estimated for year.

The return on capital employed is estimated at 2.0 per cent for the current year and has never bettered 11.0 per cent during the period under review. It needs to be recognized, also, that the returns shown are exaggerated to the extent that the level of capital employed is significantly understated due to the inclusion of fixed assets at book value rather than current value.

Whereas turnover of capital employed has remained relatively constant at 4.6 to 5.0 times per annum, margins on sales have fluctuated considerably and never bettered 2.3 per cent. In the current and preceding year margins on sales have been less than 1 per cent. Thus the picture which emerges of ABCO's overall performance is one of low growth and inadequate and declining profits and profitability.

Although the level of profits regarded as necessary to maintain and develop a business is essentially a management decision, it would seem

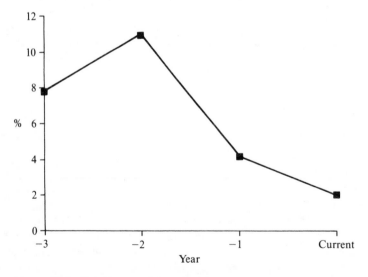

Figure 10.1 *Return on capital employed*

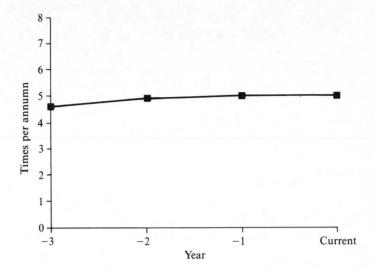

Figure 10.2 *Turnover of capital*

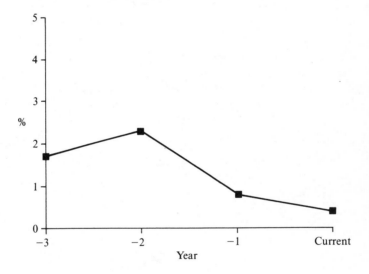

Figure 10.3 *Pre-tax profit to sales*

desirable that a business such as ABCO achieves a return on capital of at least 20 per cent in order to provide for its maintenance in real terms and produce a reasonable return to its shareholders in the process. Moreover, taking into account the nature of the business, ABCO needs to turn over its capital more than five times per annum and make at least 4 per cent profit on sales in the process.

Thus, given ABCO's recent performance, the shortfall in its profits appears to lie in the region of £100 000 per annum—i.e. the level necessary to generate returns on capital in excess of 20 per cent. At this stage of the analysis, the key to achieving it would appear to be that of finding ways to improve margins on sales first and sales volume second.

One is left wondering as to the extent to which these needs are currently reflected in the company's training plans.

Operating and financial management performance ratios

The analysis of ABCO's overall management performance ratios points to the need for improvement in both profit margins and turnover of capital employed. Ratio analysis under both headings will therefore need to be carried out in order to isolate more closely the company's problems and identify the areas where training is likely to be particularly worthwhile.

The figures in Table 10.5 show selected ratios for ABCO and appear to offer further insights into the company's position. (See also Figs 10.4, 10.5, 10.6 and 10.7.) Making allowances for inflation, it would seem that ABCO is experiencing a decline in sales revenue in real terms. Clearly, this raises questions about the company's marketing ability.

Table 10.5 *Selected operating performance ratios for ABCO*

| | Year | | | |
	−3	−2	−1	Current (9 months)
Sales growth (%)	5.3	10.1	5.2	2.3
Pre-tax profit to sales (%)	1.7	2.3	0.8	0.4
Added value to sales (%)	27.3	28.5	31.1	32.4
Wages to added value (%)	39.5	39.1	42.2	47.5
Added value per £ wages (£)	2.53	2.46	2.37	2.10
Sales per £ wages (£)	9.25	8.93	7.63	6.49

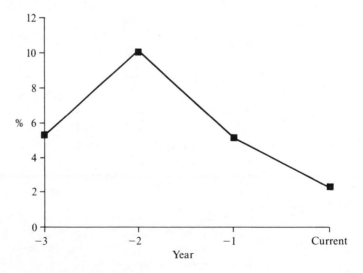

Figure 10.4 *Sales growth*

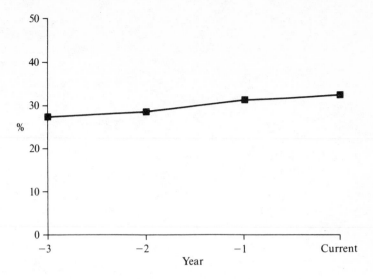

Figure 10.5 *Added value as a percentage of sales*

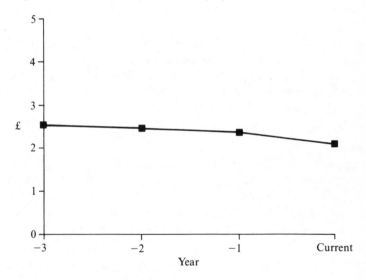

Figure 10.6 *Added value per £ wages*

It is also interesting to note the apparent relationship between sales growth and pre-tax profits—it would seem that profitability is substantially influenced by changes in sales volume. This suggests that the company may have a particular problem in controlling its costs in line with output. It also points to the need to examine the extent to which the company's cost structure makes it vulnerable to changes in sales volume.

Despite the adverse trends in sales and profitability, it can be seen that the ratio of added value to sales has been improving. At first sight, this appears positive, especially for the workforce. It could, for example, be the result of a number of factors such as an increased ability to pass on

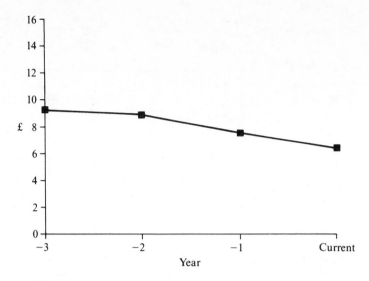

Figure 10.7   *Sales per £ wages*

material cost increases or reduced material input prices. However, if this were the case, it seems strange that the benefits have not fed through into profits. Nor would it seem to be supported by the relatively high rate of stock turnover (see Table 10.9). Instead, it would seem much more likely that these improvements are the results of underlying changes in the product mix calling for different inputs of materials and labour.

Even so, for a company that aims to offer a high level of service to its customers, it is difficult to see that the ratio of added value to sales is really sufficient to serve as a basis for running the business. This raises important questions about ABCO's marketing policy and the way in which planning of the business is conducted.

It also raises questions about the way in which ABCO buys and controls material costs. It can be reckoned, for example, that, since materials represent some 70 per cent of total costs, even a small improvement in buying performance or material utilization will have a very significant impact on profits and profitability.

The next ratio shown is that of wages to added value, and it can be seen that this is on an upward trend. The reasons for this require further investigation to assess whether, for example, it is due to changes in the product mix or reflective of ABCO's ability to control wage costs in line with sales volume. However, whatever the underlying cause, the subsequent ratios showing added value and sales per £ wages point to the conclusion that wage costs appear to be increasing at a faster rate than can be sustained by the company's current level of business.

Taking stock at this point, a number of issues can be isolated for further investigation. These raise fundamental questions about ABCO's

ability, and hence skills, in marketing, buying and controlling costs and
productivity.

Main elements of cost

Table 10.6 shows an analysis of ABCO's main element of costs. (See
also Fig. 10.8.) The costs relating to materials and wages have already
been subject to examination. Even so, it is interesting to note the sum of
these two costs. It could be concluded that they reflect a measure of
control, to some extent negating the earlier observation about ratio of
wages to added value. However, it is important to note that after these
costs have been incurred, and assuming that a pre-tax profit of 5 per
cent is to be aimed for, there is less than 15 per cent to cover all the
remaining costs.

Table 10.6 *ABCO's main elements of costs*

	Year			
	−3	−2	−1	Current (9 months)
Materials	72.7	72.5	68.9	67.6
Wages	10.8	11.2	13.1	15.4
*Selling**	3.1	3.2	6.5	6.0
Distribution	1.8	2.0	2.5	3.3
Administration †	5.9	4.5	3.7	3.4
Directors' emoluments	3.3	3.1	2.7	2.5
Other	0.7	1.2	1.8	1.4
Pre-tax profit	1.7	2.3	0.8	0.4
Sales	100	100	100	100

* Includes directors' commission.
† Includes overdraft finance costs.

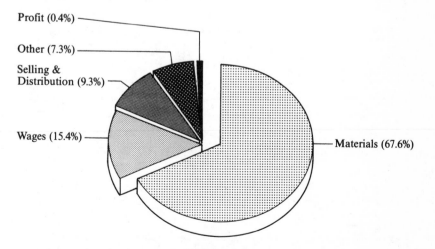

Figure 10.8 *ABCO's current cost structure*

The pattern of these remaining costs provides a number of pointers. It can be seen that administration costs appear to have been brought increasingly under control. Against this, the costs of selling and distribution show an adverse trend. When added together, selling and distribution costs show an increase from 4.9 per cent of sales in year $t-3$ to 9.3 per cent in the current year. It could therefore be argued that this largely explains ABCO's shortfall in profits.

Given the recent sales performance of the company, the increase in selling costs would appear to be a particular cause for concern. In absolute terms, however, they are not necessarily excessive, particularly since they include an element of directors' remuneration. Even so, for every pound ABCO is spending, they appear to be getting less value for their money in terms of sales generated. The effectiveness of these activities therefore requires close examination.

Given, also, the narrowness of the margins on which the company is operating, it follows that control of costs throughout the business is of great importance. The overall impression provided by ABCO's main elements of cost ratios does not really present a convincing picture that the level of control is sufficient.

At one level this can be seen as a reflection of ABCO's administrative skills. More fundamentally, however, on the basis of the other information that has been gathered, it would seem to suggest that the company may be lacking the appropriate skills in business planning. If this is so, it implies major changes in the way in which the business is designed and managed. In the process, training will be required not just to ensure implementation but also to make sound decisions upon which to base the changes.

Other elements of cost

Other useful insights into a ABCO's performance can be gained by examining fixed and variable costs. For example, in noting the apparent relationship between sales growth and pre-tax profits, it was observed that the company may have a particular problem in controlling its costs in line with output. Among other things, this pointed to the need to examine the extent to which the company's cost structure made it vulnerable to changes in sales volume.

An analysis based on ABCO's fixed and variable costs is shown in Table 10.7. (See also Fig. 10.9.) ABCO's current position is reflected in column 2, where sales for the year of £2.5 million are expected to result in an operating profit of £10 000. Against this, it can be seen that if sales were to decline by 20 per cent a loss of more than £100 000 would result. However, an increase in sales of 20 per cent from the current level would result in a thirteenfold increase in profits to a much more satisfactory level. This would seem to put the need to review ABCO's marketing skills into a very relevant context!

By breaking down these costs further (for example, into direct and indirect costs according to products and markets), it is possible to form a

Table 10.7 *Contribution analysis—ABCO*

Sales (£000's)	2000	**2500**	3000	3500
Variable costs	1500	**1875**	2250	2625
Contribution	500	**625**	750	875
Fixed costs	615	**615**	615	615
Profit/(loss)	(115)	**10**	135	260

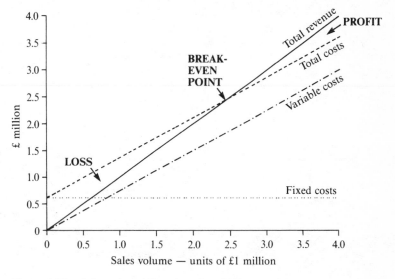

Figure 10.9 *Sales vulnerability chart for ABCO*

view on which activities are really generating satisfactory returns or otherwise. This is particularly valuable where resources are scarce and, from a training perspective, can help in making decisions as to whether to invest training effort in improving unsatisfactory performance or building upon evident strengths.

An example of this sort of analysis is given in Table 10.8. This shows the added value achieved by ABCO from sales of its different product groups in different markets. (See also Fig. 10.10.)

From the table it can be seen that product group A accounts for appoximately 70 per cent of sales. However, because of its relatively low rate of contribution (25.5 per cent), it produces only 55 per cent of the overall contribution.

Product group D produces the highest rate of contribution—63.2 per cent compared with the average for all product groups of 32.4 per cent. Although sales of this product group are a relatively modest 14.5 per cent of total sales, it provides 28.2 per cent of the total contribution. Market 3 accounts for the bulk of sales (70 per cent) and profits (63.8 per cent). Market 2, although relatively small (12 per cent of total sales), yields a relatively high contribution of 45.7 per cent.

Table 10.8　Contribution analysis of ABCO's sales by product and market

Product group/market		1	2	3	Total	
	(£000's)					
A	Sales	248	58	1059	1365	70.6
	Contribution	63	15	270	348	55.5
	%				25.5	
B	Sales	11	61	162	234	12.1
	Contribution	4	23	61	88	14.0
	%				37.6	
C	Sales	7	9	38	54	2.8
	Contribution	2	2	10	14	2.2
	%				25.9	
D	Sales	82	104	94	280	14.5
	Contribution	52	66	59	177	28.2
	%				63.2	
Total	Sales	348	232	1353	1933	100
	Contribution	121	106	400	627	100
	%	34.8	45.7	29.6	32.4	
% all sales		18.0	12.0	70.0		
% all contributions		19.3	16.9	63.8		

Note: this analysis is based on the direct cost of materials only.

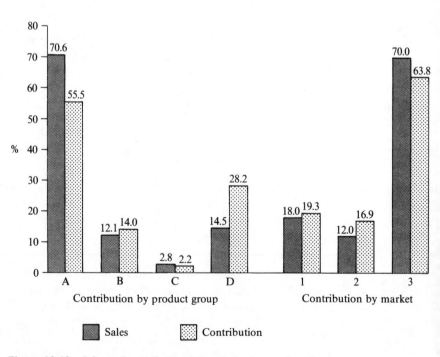

Figure 10.10　*Sales and contribution by product group and market*

In broad terms, it would seem that low margins are associated with high-volume product groups. It may be that this is a reflection of ABCO's traditional source of business. The contribution from product group D in market 2 seems particularly worth noting.

Drawing further conclusions from this analysis is extremely difficult and risky without further information (for example, relating to ABCO's markets and the associated direct costs of servicing them). However, at face value, the figures suggest that priority should be given to directing training efforts towards:

1 The improvement of profitability of product group A, and
2 Volume expansion of product group D (e.g. through developing new business)

More generally, the analysis raises a number of questions. For example:

• Why is it that product prices are not differentiated according to different markets?
• Why is it that for product group D the level of sales across the different market appears relatively even?
• How are marketing and sales objectives and targets set?
• How are sales resources determined and allocated?
• What is the training provision and how does it relate to the marketing and sales objectives?

Thus it can be seen that contribution analysis provides a very sound basis upon which to raise many questions about a company's sales and marketing policies and the associated skills and the level of training provision. In addition, it also provides pointers which can be extremely helpful and potentially very rewarding when deciding where and how training investment will be most profitably allocated.

Financial performance ratios

Table 10.9 shows the financial performance ratios for ABCO over a three-year period. (See also Figs 10.11, 10.12 and 10.13.) The figures for the current year are not shown here, since they relate to a different point in time of the company's trading year and are not therefore really

Table 10.9 *ABCO's financial operating performance*

	Year −3	Year −2	Year −1
Turnover of working capital	10.6	11.7	**12.5**
Current ratio	2.0	1.8	**1.9**
Acid test	1.8	1.7	**1.8**
Debtors—days outstanding	62	60	**54**
Creditors—days outstanding	31	15	**15**
Stocks—days in hand	5	5	**4**

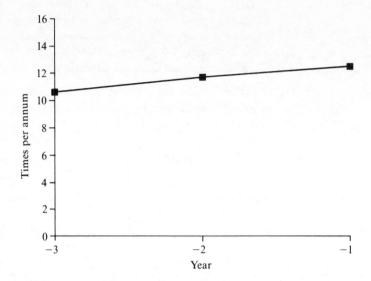

Figure 10.11   *Turnover of working capital*

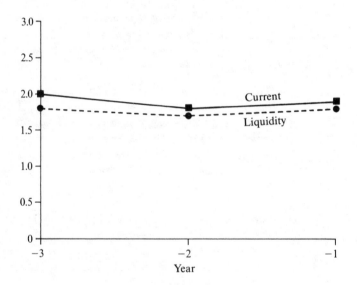

Figure 10.12   *Current and liquidity ratios*

comparable. It can be seen that turnover of working capital has increased steadily, reflecting its improved utilization. The current and acid test ratios are relatively constant and suggest a healthy position in terms of both solvency and liquidity.

Turning to the working capital components, the progressive decline in days of debt outstanding would seem to reflect a continuous improvement and has to be seen as positive. However, given the significance of debtors, i.e. £386 862 at the end of $t-1$, and the implicit associated finance costs, it is clearly going to be important to review the effectiveness of training arrangements for the control of debtors.

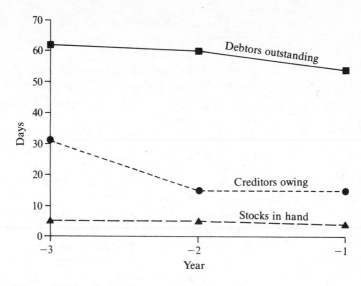

Figure 10.13 Stocks, debtors and creditors

The trend in the creditors ratio would also seem to be positive. It suggests, when compared with the number of days' stocks in hand, that a change in policy and a more consistent approach has been adopted.

It is interesting to consider the creditor and debtor ratios together. This seems to suggest that the terms of credit on which the company buys compares unfavourably with those on which it sells. An important implication which follows from this is that any expansion in sales volume is likely to have to be supported by further improvements in debtors' control or an increase in borrowing. Given the managing director's policy on financial control and cash management, the immediate prospects of the latter would seem remote. This adds even more weight to the importance of assessing training arrangements in credit management.

Summary and conclusions

From a training perspective, the main findings of this analysis of ABCO's financial ratios can be summarized as follows:

- The business appears to be adequately capitalized and its balance sheet strong. However, internally generated funds are insufficient to provide adequately for the maintenance and development of the business. This is resulting in a steady erosion of capital in real terms.
- The company is, to all intents and purposes, operating at its break-even point. Although there are indications that profits could be improved very substantially for relatively modest improvements in performance, ABCO is also vulnerable to incur substantial losses should improved performance not be achieved.
- The current level of shortfall in profits would seem to be in excess of £100 000 per annum. To remedy this, there is evidently a need to increase the turnover of capital, i.e. sales volume and the margin

made on sales in the process. This clearly raises questions about the company's abilities and skills in:

1 Marketing and selling
2 Controlling costs in line with output

- Since materials account for almost 70 per cent of total costs, the company needs to ensure that its skills in buying and materials control are particularly strong.
- Administration costs appear to have been brought increasingly under control. Even so, the amount of working capital tied up in debtors implies the need to ensure that the system, task allocation and associated training arrangements are particularly effective.
- Considering the improvements in the control of administration costs, together with those reflected in the working capital and financial operating performance ratios, would seem to suggest a reservoir of skills. These skills might usefully be applied elsewhere in the business.
- The overall picture presented by the analysis suggests that the company may be lacking in the skills of business planning. In turn, this may have implications for the way in which the organization is structured and managed.
- Training investment needs to be directed towards improving both the overall and operating management performance of the company. This has implications for the short- and long-term planning of training. However, before these needs can be prioritized and planned for, further information is necessary. This can only be obtained by looking behind the figures.

11 Behind the figures: organization review

Introduction   So far, readers should have been able to follow the analysis of ABCO without too much difficulty and without feeling too remote from its business activity. It has, after all, centred around the analysis of hard data in order to build a picture of the company's overall financial structure and performance.

In gathering the data and listening to the 'noise' of daily life in an organization one is picking up cues. This is both a conscious and an unconscious process and it is often only on reflection, or as the picture builds up, that their significance becomes apparent and shapes the direction and interpretation of the process of enquiry.

In examining ABCO's financial performance it may be that you are frustrated at the conditionality of some of the analysis. Alternatively, you may have drawn different conclusions from the same data. Don't be put off by this—there are few absolutes. Much more important is an attitude of openness towards different meanings and interpretations, and a willingness to pursue different lines of enquiry as the picture unfolds. This is, after all, the point of looking behind the figures.

We have reached the point, however, at which further progress will only be made by checking out the figures and understanding the organizational processes that underlie them. This can only be achieved by talking to people—not only managers responsible for running the business but staff at all levels. It could even involve suppliers, customers or other outside agencies.

At this point, therefore, trainers need to bring all their technical and process skills into play. From this point on, too, the reader can hardly expect to play the game. However, the acid test for assessing the level and quality of this sort of analysis is the credibility of the final picture presented to the organization and the extent to which it reflects—as in a mirror—images which are helpful and free from distortion. If these qualities are not present, the preconditions of awareness and interest necessary for moving up a new learning curve are unlikely to be met. This highlights the value of adopting the approach outlined in Chapters 8 and 9. In practice, it also minimizes the time required to undertake the work. But this is only half the story, for in the process it inevitably begins to 'loosen things up'.

Thus many members of ABCO's staff who had been 'unheard' for years, if ever, began to unburden themselves and take a new interest in their function and underlying importance. Others displayed visible discomfort (particularly those whose sense of importance and security depended upon their position in the pecking order) at having to argue their case on the basis of evidence of performance rather than their relationship with the managing director. For the managing director, too, the survey carried the need to face up to perceptions about his skills and style of management and the ways in which his values and competing and separate interests impinged upon and even conflicted with the needs of ABCO.

Addressing these issues reinforces the point made earlier about the skills of the trainer. It also highlights the importance of the commitment of senior management to training discussed in Chapter 8, since it is only they who have the authority and means to promote understanding of its purpose throughout the organization and ensure the cooperation of those involved.

Organization review—the key findings

Overview

The information gathered through the financial ratio analysis provided a structured basis on which to hold discussions with managers and other key members of staff. In broad terms, the company's main strategic problem appeared to be that of achieving an adequate volume of profitable sales in order to overcome the current and continuing shortfall in profits in the region of £100 000 per annum. In turn, this could be seen as comprising both short- and medium-term needs and opportunities.

Short- and medium-term needs and opportunities

In the short term it was important that the company should focus its attention and skills on:

- Controlling material costs
- Improving the efficiency of the preparation department
- Pricing and price negotiation
- Selling skills and resources
- Major customer profitability

In the medium term, substantial improvements in the company's approach and skills in planning, organization and control across the business were necessary in order to achieve improvements in productivity.

It was also important to improve the level of personnel management and training skills in the business. The immediate reason for this was that it was apparent that employment policies, based on low basic wage rates and extensive overtime working combined with inadequate induction and basic skills training, were contributing to high levels of labour turnover, absenteeism, material wastage and poor levels of productivity.

The company also needed to give particular attention to the development of their marketing skills in order to identify more closely the market opportunities which the company could meet. Only by identifying these opportunities would the company achieve the long-term level of profitability necessary to maintain and develop the business as a whole.

Longer-term needs On a longer-term view, development at a rather more fundamental level was required. The reason for this was that, although the company appeared to have overcome some of its basic structural problems, the difficulties of working together appeared to have increased. In turn, it could be seen that these were contributing to the problems of profitably exploiting the company's policies and skills—and would continue to do so.

In particular, it was felt necessary to address the organization's underlying pattern of management and methods of operating. At one level these could be seen to be important factors adversely affecting organization effectiveness and productivity. At another, it could be anticipated that failure to address these aspects was likely to undermine the efforts and ability of the organization to develop its skills.

To put this in perspective, there was a clear lack of formal strategy. This was also manifest in the differing perceptions of the needs of the business expressed by the managing director, the marketing director and the accountant outlined in the previous chapter. Moreover, the implicit strategy which could be seen to exist was unduly shaped and influenced by the separate interests of the managing director—for example, his concern to develop the property interests of the group and limit working capital necessary for the development of ABCO in the process.

In terms of its structure, ABCO could be seen, essentially, to be organized on functional lines, with specialists appointed to specific roles (for example, sales and marketing, transport and distribution, accounting). Except the accountant, these specialists had risen within an evolving organization, rather than having been developed or recruited with professional training and specific skills for the tasks required to be accomplished in a larger organization.

In terms of its overriding culture, ABCO could be described as fitting nicely the 'power' model. The evidence for this could be gleaned from the way in which managers and staff were positioned around the managing director and the relationships between them. Further evidence was provided by the very different working conditions available to different members of the organization, including managers.

There also appeared to be a pervading style of management which made extensive use of personal and subjective evaluation, rather than more objective forms. This translated into a pattern of management akin to that of 'reward and punishment'—both material and psychological—

as a basis for maintaining control. Evidence for this view was also gleaned from observation of the gathering and use of information relating to performance and the nature of payment systems in operation.

Although such systems of management may be effective, in ABCO the particular blend of strategy, structure and culture appeared to result in a number of consequences:

- The company's management was stronger in terms of technical competence than in 'human' management skills, but relatively weak in both.
- The rate of change and standards required to maintain and develop the business was putting managers under considerable pressure, particularly where they had come up through the ranks.
- Managers lacked awareness of whether the company was making adequate profits in absolute and relative terms.
- Managers were experiencing increasing difficulty in identifying and achieving the appropriate balance between short- and medium-term priorities and needs.
- Administrative and accounting procedures had been developed to meet the *ad hoc* demands for information made by the managing director, particularly those relating to cash management and his separate interest in developing the group's property business, rather than providing a sound basis for the direction and development of ABCO.
- Although basic accounting systems appeared to have been generally well maintained and to have been developed substantially since the appointment of the new accountant, the general level of information available for day-to-day use by operating management was extremely limited. Besides being reflective of attitudes to information, decision making and control systems in general, this lack of information also constituted a serious weakness and potential threat to the company.
- Whereas the managing director was, at times, actively and vociferously concerned to improve margins and reduce wastage and losses, operating managers were limited in their ability to contribute to this, not just as a result of insufficient information with which to control costs but also due to their lack of involvement in budgeting.
- Managers rarely met together as a group and, when they did, there was little open discussion or participation. A number of managers also tended to be excluded from meetings, thereby further restricting information and heightening the sense of self-interest, conflict and anxiety.
- A general attitude of defensiveness pervaded throughout the organization, manifesting itself in the justification of action/inaction. In turn, this resulted in a tendency to attribute shortfalls in performance to others, rather than seeking cooperative solutions to the problems facing the business.

Conclusion

It was evident that not only was training essential for developing the company's skills in line with the changing needs of the business, it could also contribute significantly to the development of the business as a whole. In the process, it would contribute to the strengthening of its financial structure, financial performance, marketing, purchasing, preparation, distribution and personnel functions. However, before this could take place it would be important to gain acceptance of the needs that had been identified.

Bringing about change to improve this sort of situation is notoriously difficult. At one level, increasing awareness of the situation and the unproductive and destructive circularity which results can be helpful. At another, it is perhaps best addressed indirectly by establishing structures which in turn affect behaviour. This has particular implications for the planning and design of training and the provision of associated support.

In this sort of setting, Action Learning approaches (see Chapter 8) can be very helpful. Besides putting responsibility for training where it belongs, it is a good way of involving people in the change process. With the support of the managing director a meeting of ABCO's senior staff, including the union convenor, was called. Following a presentation and discussion of the findings of the survey it was agreed to:

1 Allocate responsibilities for dealing with the short- and medium-term problems faced by the business to specific managers or groups.
2 Clarify and agree their objectives and responsibilities with them against such headings as:
   —Major needs
   —People involved
   —Training objectives and methods
   —Time scales
   —Expected costs and benefits.
3 Ensure that they were aware of the necessary information, knowledge and skills to fulfil them.
4 Establish methods and time scales for monitoring and reviewing progress.
5 Provide appropriate support.

Within this framework it was recognized that it would also be very important to strike a sensible balance between short- and long-term strategies. For example, in the short term, training needed to be effective in contributing to immediate improvements in performance and results. By doing so, it would demonstrate the value of training and provide encouragement to do more. In the longer term, to bring about a more permanent change and consistent attitudes to training, it would be necessary to address the deep-seated problems within the company.

COMPANY'S MAIN PROBLEM/ OPPORTUNITY	PEOPLE INVOLVED	TRAINING METHOD
(A) *ACHIEVING ADEQUATE VOLUME OF* *PROFITABLE SALES*		
(1) Major customer profitability	Managing Director Sales Director Accountant Consultant	Task group Selected reading On-the-job counselling
(2) Product and market profitability		
(3) Development of pricing structure		
(4) Development of profitable sales	Managing Director Sales Director Sales and Telesales staff	(1) Phased attendance on 3-day external workshops on negotiation skills in selling. (2) On-the-job training, including accompanied calls. (3) Training skills workshop for telesales supervisor.
(5) Increase sales volume	Appointment of 2 new salespersons. (Possibly 1 from telesales and 1 redundant national/major accounts salesperson. Telesales replacement would suit bright school leaver or returner to work.)	(1) Off-the-job sales training according to individual needs, e.g. selling skills, advanced/ refresher training. (2) On-the-job training, including accompanied calls. (3) Development of company sales training manual by consultant, sales director and salespersons.
(6) Identification of market opportunities for the company's products and services.	Managing Director Sales Director Marketing Assistant (new appointment recommended, ideal post for a graduate trainee).	Integrated in-company, on-the-job training programme.
(B) *IMPROVEMENT OF GROSS MARGINS* *ON FRESH PRODUCE*	Managing Director Buyer Warehouse Manager Preparation Dept Manager Transport Manager Accountant Union representative	Dependent upon findings of internal investigation into working practices and procedures. On-the-job training in new procedures and standards likely to be required.
(C) *IMPROVE COST CONTROL*	All directors and managers	Counselling of individual line managers and directors by accountant.
(D) *IMPROVE GENERAL LEVEL OF* *INFORMATION FOR DAY-TO-DAY* *USE OF OPERATING MANAGEMENT* (Exploration phase)	All directors and managers, selected staff from all departments.	Selected reading. In-company information technology appreciation seminar. Attendance at exhibitions. Discussions with selected packaged systems producers and consultants.

Figure 12.1   ABCO's Training Plan

OBJECTIVES	TIME SCALE	EXPECTED BENEFITS	EXPECTED COSTS
Evaluate performance and potential for improvement	Months 1–3 Completion by November		
As above	Months 2–4 Completion by December	Increased profitability of existing business.	Course fees and expenses £2300 Consultant's fees £5200
Design profitable pricing structure	Months 2–6 Completion by February	Additional 3% return on sales.	
Introduce new pricing structure	Months 2–9 Completion by May		
Development of 10% new business per year for 3 years.	6–18 months	Increase in turnover of capital employed by 20% to 6 in Year 2; maintained thereafter. Improvement in net return on sales of 2%.	Figures for expected benefits struck *after* providing additional selling expenses to cover salary, commission travel and overhead expenses. Phased increase in staffing levels (telesales, preparation, warehouse and transport department of 4 in Year 2 and 3 in Year 3. Consultant fees and training manual development £3800.
Development of marketing and sales information data base and preparation of continuous assessments of performance and market opportunities for the company's products and services.	1–3 years	Enhanced ability to achieve and maintain long-term levels of profitability in order to maintain and develop the business as a whole.	£12 000 in Year 1 rising to £20 000 in Year 3.
Reduce wastage and rate of issue of credit notes.	0–6 months	2% improvement in gross margins on fresh produce.	Dependent on findings of investigation. Suggest provision of £3500 to develop and introduce new training standards in ware-house procedures.
Development of existing budgetary control system.	6 months to 3 years	Enhanced ability and skills to control costs, develop budgets, plan for contingencies and balance short- and medium-term priorities and needs.	Provision of £1000 course fees for accountant to develop advisory/counselling skills. Expect to provide £6000 p.a. during Year 2 and £12 000 thereafter to appoint accounting trainee to assist accountant.
Increased awareness of potential contribution of information-processing systems and methods relative to the company's day-to-day needs, and, in the medium term, improving approaches to planning, organization and control at the functional and overall levels.	6–15 months	Enhanced ability to introduce, maintain and develop cost-effective information systems.	Seminar costs etc. £1500. Provide for £1200 for initial study prior to commissioning feasibility survey to assess and introduce improved methods of information processing.

12 Getting results

Planning the training

Figure 12.1 shows the plan developed with ABCO to bring about change. Central to its development was the recognition of the need for staff, particularly senior managers, to work better together. In this sense, the activity of allocating responsibilities, determining objectives and methods of achievement provided a helpful blend of task and process activity. It also served as a vehicle for the managing director to play a more active and supportive role in the day-to-day operational management of the business.

From the work of the various groups two issues quickly emerged as holding particular importance and potential. One of these related to the need to improve the control of costs, the other to the need to expand sales volume.

Control of costs

The issue of the control of costs related particularly to materials. As a percentage of sales these had been averaging more than 67 per cent. In a business which aimed to offer a high level of service that seemed to be very high. Something had to be done.

In thinking of ways in which training affects material costs, one possible starting point was to look at the buying function—often something of a Cinderella in many organizations. If ABCO could improve its buying performance by 1 per cent, it would double its profits. So at the very least, it would be important to check out the extent to which those responsible for buying had been trained in buying and negotiation skills and others in the department in order processing.

Then there was warehousing and stock control. To what extent was produce received into the warehouse in line with that ordered in terms of both quantity and quality? Within the warehouse, which included ripening rooms, what was the level of care exercised in stock rotation, handling perishable commodities and order picking? How were staff trained to do this? Did it include awareness of the various costs of different sorts of produce?

Food preparation inevitably involves wastage, but the level is primarily dependent upon the quality of produce being worked upon, the attitudes towards it of those working on it and the knife skills they possess. It may seem surprising, but peeling potatoes involves a much higher degree of skill than is generally recognized. Skilled operators achieve considerably higher levels of output than their less skilled counterparts through the manual dexterity they possess and their ability to 'plan the potato'. They also create less wastage in the process—an example of how speed and quality can come together. The same applies to the preparation of other vegetables and fruit salads, though the costs involved are generally of a much greater order.

From a more general perspective, if management freely and openly help themselves to produce, particularly to see themselves, their families and even their friends through the weekend, is it surprising if those actually working with the produce feel entitled to tuck some away on their own account? It all adds up and, in time, becomes deep-rooted in the culture of the business. How much, one might wonder, had this to do with the attitude underlying the managing director's chagrin at his 'missing 4 per cent'?

More than this, the control of costs can be examined in the context of pricing. For example, is the organization charging enough for its products? Is it aware of the costs of different materials and reasonable allowances for weight loss and other forms of wastage? Is it aware of the profitability of each product line? Underlying these issues are a whole range of possibilities ranging from skills in marketing to those of cost accounting and the application of information technology.

Exploration in each of these areas led to a range of courses of action. A good example is provided by the Preparation Department, where it was found that productivity was poor and deteriorating. Contributing to this it was found that:

- Skill shortages were acute—the department was operating with 30 per cent fewer staff than the level of work called for.
- As a result, the hours being worked were long. Operators were expected to work in the region of 70 hours per week and up to 7 days a week. Discussions with the local office of the Department of Employment indicated just how much the company's conditions of employment were below those of their competitors and how unaware management were of the problem.
- Labour turnover was very high—well over 100 per cent per annum—adding to the pressure on staff to work even longer hours. There was no shortage of job applicants and many offers were made—but less than one in ten started, and for those that did, a typical staying time before leaving was no more than 2 days.
- Wastage rates were high and an increasing number of customer complaints and returns indicated that quality of both product and service (e.g. late deliveries) was deteriorating.
- Training for new operators could, at best, be described as rudimentary, a result not least of the disdain which the supervisor and senior/long-service operators appeared to show towards new members of the department. In cultural terms this was not so different from that pervading the whole company. However, as a result, training times—for

those who made it—were long, amounting to more than 300 hours lost production just to acquire basic knife skills. Even those who were eager to learn were obstructed by the failure of those with responsibility for training to impart all the knowledge necessary to do any particular task, on the one hand, and give adequate feedback on performance, on the other.

Training design

This system has been developed with the objective of minimizing learning times for new entrants to the department.

The system concentrates on:

1 Peeling potatoes
2 Pommes Chateau
3 Pommes Parisienne.

These operations have been selected because they represent approximately 70% of the departmental hours worked. Additionally, compared with other produce such as fruit salads prepared by the department, the material cost of potatoes is relatively low, thereby minimizing wastage costs during training.

The programme takes into account the need for the trainee to produce output from the first day of his/her employment and to reduce labour costs and labour turnover. It is estimated that a new entrant of average ability should be able to achieve a satisfactory level of performance within 4 to 6 weeks of joining and at a cost of no more than 150 hours lost production.[1]

It is expected that there will be a high transfer of skills element to all other jobs in the department involving knife skills, except those calling for chopping. Even in the jobs involving chopping there is expected to be a transfer of skills because of the trainee's familiarity with materials and their textures, a range of cutting tools, and the development of manual dexterity, stamina and perception.

The system has been prepared by:

1 Carrying out a skills analysis of a range of activities;
2 Examining differences between fast and slow workers;
3 Deriving training syllabae;
4 Preparing training programmes, complete with instruction notes and visual aids;

After initial induction, skills training should commence with peeling potatoes. Training on Pommes Parisienne should also start on the first day in order to provide variety and develop manual dexterity. Because of the high risk of wastage, training on Pommes Chateau should not be introduced until the trainee has demonstrated a basic competence in peeling potatoes.

Training should commence off-the-job, i.e. at a separate work table from the main preparation area. This will enable trainees to acquire basic knowledge and skills before transferring to the on-the-job situation where they can concentrate on building up speed and stamina.

Trainers

Trainers using this system should have received training as instructors to the level of at least that offered by a basic Job Instruction Course. This will enable them to:

—understand the techniques and principles upon which this manual is based;
—develop their instructional skills;
—provide feedback on performance in a way that is helpful to trainees;
—make further and continuous improvements to the training system.

Note

1 In practice, a target time of 100 hours should be realistic and achievable by most operators.

Figure 12.2   Extract from the food-preparation training manual

Figure 12.2 shows an extract from the training system developed for the food-preparation department and designed to remedy some of the problems of low productivity.

Expanding sales volume

The second major issue involved the need to expand sales volume. However, gaining acceptance of this by the managing director took a great deal of persuasion by the project team. It seemed that he was so locked into the notion of his 'missing 4 per cent' and the control of cash that he was effectively blind to the other needs facing the business stemming from the decline in sales volume in real terms and declining productivity per pound of wages. Together, these were seriously under-mining the company's cost structure and making it increasingly sensitive to small changes in volume (see vulnerability analysis, Table 10.7).

Part of the change in attitude was brought about by the progress of the team working on the issue of improving the control of costs. However, it was much enhanced by the growing awareness that the company's performance was not being limited by a single issue and that a mix of strategies was required to bring about the necessary improvements. As a result, the managing director came to see that, in fact his 'missing 4 per cent' was a function of both the control of costs and sales volume. This awareness was sufficient for him to realize the potential value of switching resources into the sales operation and investing in its profes-sional development. Figure 12.3 shows an extract from the sales training manual developed to provide practical help, on the one hand, and con-sistency with ABCO's strategy, structure and culture, on the other.

Introduction

The company has been built up by providing best quality fresh produce combined with the highest level of service to the hotel and catering trades. The product range has been complemented by prepared, frozen and dry produce.

Your company is first and foremost in the business of achieving adequate returns on capital employed in order to maintain and develop its ability to meet perceived market needs and opportunities. In doing so it aims to maintain a balance between the interests of its shareholders, board of directors, employees and customers.

The establishment of a sales force actively engaged in the development of new business represents a new phase in the development of the company. Its success depends primarily on your ability, skills and motivation to achieve maximum profitable sales volume within the markets and policies defined by the company. In turn, this requires that the company provides you with a sound framework for operating, developing your performance and realizing your personal goals.

In developing this framework to meet the overall needs of the business, the company recognizes the importance of involving its employees and drawing upon their experience. We aim to evolve a system which is constantly live and changing, but clearly understood.

You are joining the company at an early stage in the re-vitalization of the selling system and the formation of a professional selling operation. You therefore have an excellent opportunity to enjoy and contribute to its development now and in the future.

The following pages provide for the foundation of this process by setting out key aspects of:

—your job
—background knowledge
—product, service and technical knowledge
—hotel and catering industry information
—company strategy, policies and procedures
—selling methods and techniques
—selling skills

The aim is to provide a series of important discussion points between you and the company and which we hope will be helpful in working together.

Figure 12.3   Extract from sales training manual

Evaluation

Evaluation presents problems for most trainers. As a result, in most organizations, training investment decisions are more an act of faith, closely allied to depth of conviction held by senior management of the need for training, rather than a response to evaluation. In this sense, by putting monetary values on potential training investment decisions, the Training for Profit approach provides a logical as well as persuasive basis for evaluating training needs.

However, evaluation needs to go deeper than this. On the one hand, it involves assessing the extent to which training has been carried out efficiently: on the other, it raises the question of whether it was worth the investment.

It could be argued that most organizations do not have the resources or skills to carry out this activity in any great depth. Others would claim that, particularly in assessing effectiveness, because of the whole range of variables involved it is not possible to assess the training contribution separate from other factors affecting performance. With an approach such as Training for Profit and its function as an integrating mechanism, precise evaluation becomes even more difficult. Realistically, this can only be done by considering the sorts of results achieved in fairly broad terms and over a period of time.

At ABCO, as might be expected, a review of progress 12 months following completion of the overall assessment of training needs reflected different levels of success across the various programmes and departments. However, specific results included:

- The telesales operation had increased sales by more than 20 per cent.
- Sales of prepared produce, the company's most profitable product group, had increased by 50 per cent.
- The managing director was satisfied that gross profit margins could not be improved further except by making major changes in business policy and practice.
- The new budgeting system had been introduced and accepted by departmental managers. It was resulting in active discussion.
- There was acknowledgement that a shift in the company's approach to decision making had taken place, evidenced by increased levels of investigation and preparation prior to implementation of initiatives.

Interestingly, also, the increase in the level of sales volume and its associated impact on the workloads, resources and skills of other departments was creating its own problems. This was resulting in the consideration of the appointment of additional staff to review and monitor company activities on a more consistent and permanent basis and to ensure that all employee matters were related to the needs and developments of the company.

Evaluating the development of ABCO's training system in terms of process, it could be said that, in general terms, it was:

- More systematic, in that there was evidence of planning and the selection of some major business areas for treatment
- Focused on organizational effectiveness
- Resulting in higher levels of investment and commitment
- Contributing to positive trends and results
- Serving as an integrating mechanism, by providing a linkage between the approach to assessing training needs and the results achieved

At the same time, it has to be recognized that ABCO is still a very long way from having a durable, systematic and fully integrated training system. For this to be achieved, one would expect to see evidence over a longer time period and the development, for example, of:

- Continuing commitment from the managing director and the definition and acceptance of responsibility for training throughout the business
- Training policy, including the statement of priorities, goals and key performance indicators
- Information and processes for gathering and analysing training needs
- Regular reviews of employee performance as a basis for the assessment of individual training and development needs
- 'Basic training' for all employees
- Supplementary training and development programmes for different categories of employees
- An incentive system to encourage positive attitudes to training and development—for example, pre-conditions for promotions and upgrading, pay awards and bands related to the acquisition of skills
- Follow-up arrangements to reinforce both on- and off-the-job training
- Training resources, including the development of training skills across the company and access to skills from alternative sources, in order to ensure appropriate quality standards
- Training budgets
- Evaluation of training investment covering all of these areas and examples of the results achieved through training.[1]

Note

1 This provides a context in which to consider the 'Investors in People' approach being promoted in Britain by the Employment Department and Training and Enterprise Councils. The starting point for the scheme is the perception that although 'the crucial importance of people to business is now almost universally recognised by companies . . . there is a huge gap between recognising this, and knowing exactly what to do about it'. (*Investors in People: A Brief for Top Managers*, Employment Department, 1991, p.1). Stemming from this is the development of a national standard based on the framework that an Investor in People:

1 Makes a public commitment from the top to develop all employees to achieve its business objectives
2 Regularly reviews the training and development needs of all employees
3 Takes action to train people on recruitment and throughout their employment
4 Evaluates the investment in training and development to assess achievement and improve future effectiveness

Conclusion to Part Five

The aim of this part of the book has been to provide an example of the Training for Profit approach in action. It began with a preliminary examination of ABCO's financial results, which suggested that the company was finding progress difficult. There appeared to be insufficient internally generated funds to provide adequately for the development of the business.

The next step was to conduct a more detailed financial appraisal using the techniques of ratio analysis. This resulted in the identification of a number of issues for further investigation and led to discussions being held with those involved—not just managers responsible for running the business but staff at all levels. It also involved talking with outside agencies.

In broad terms, the review showed how training could contribute to the development of skills in line with the changing needs of the business. Properly planned and managed, it offered a means to improve the company's financial structure and performance, while also strengthening its marketing, purchasing, preparation, distribution and personnel functions.

To achieve this, an Action Learning approach was adopted on the basis that, apart from putting responsibility for training where it belonged (i.e. with management) it would also be a good way of involving members of the workforce in the change process. It also enabled the managing director to play a more active and supportive role in the day-to-day operational management of the business and provided opportunities for managers and staff to learn to work better together.

Some questions you might like to consider could include:

Does the approach provide or suggest a framework which could be developed and applied to meet the needs of your situation?
What difficulties might arise in adopting it?
How could these difficulties be overcome?
What sorts of benefits might result?
What action needs to be taken?

PART SIX

Conclusion

Introduction

In evaluating the training system at ABCO, it was noted that the company was still a very long way from having one that was durable, systematic and fully integrated with the business. In larger organizations in particular, regarding the assessment of training needs, trainer's could, justifiably ask (or be asked!) the question: What sort of things should we be doing? In conclusion, therefore, this final part of the book aims to review a range of contemporary issues and assess their significance for the assessment of training needs.

13 Training for a profitable future

The changing environment

So, what sort of things should trainers be doing? This is a most difficult question to answer—not just because the answer is necessarily organization-specific but also because trainers and organizations are faced with an acute dilemma: at a time when the rate of change in the environment is ever increasing they have to develop long-term strategies for the future. Examples of such changes include:

- Shorter product life cycles as a result of more rapid development of new products
- Technological developments leading to changes in products and processes
- Greater exposure of domestic markets to competitors with 'world-class' ability and ambitions
- Rapidly changing competitive conditions resulting from fluctuations in financial exchange rates
- More intense and focused competition leading to increasing pressure to find new ways to add value, raise productivity and cut costs
- The surge of political and social interest in environmental protection and the growing influence of the economic theory of sustainable development

The combined effects of these changes are such that the rapid adaptation and acquisition of skills can be seen to be the key to sustaining competitive advantage. This is how Renato Riverso, President-Directeur General of IBM Europe, puts it:

The rules of the business game are changing. But the cause is not just 1992, or the democratization of Central Europe, or even the new world order which seems to be evolving before our eyes, though each of these is having its own impact. It goes much deeper. For it seems to me that in practically every sector of the economy, the dynamics of competition are shifting away from the industrial logic of the past to the service-driven philosophy of the future.

The difference is simple. Industrial logic is about the perfection of the process. It culminates in the perfect product being delivered to the customer. Service philosophy begins with the manufacture and delivery of the product, and then builds on it. So it is not a substitution, but an extra dimension to business (Riverso, 1992, p.3).

All these elements impact upon the members of a workforce in terms of their attitude and ability to keep abreast of developments, maintain and expand their knowledge and develop their skills. They also impact upon formal careers (for example, in the professions) in that the time required to introduce changes can be very long.

This is why, to be effective, training plans need to relate to the organization as a whole, not just the specific needs facing individuals or groups within it. This also carries the implication that for most organizations a mix of training strategies will be far more effective than one of universal application. Only by doing so will a sufficient degree of integration be achieved.

The difficulties in achieving this level of integration cannot be overstated. For example, in the period 1955–80 almost one company in two in *Fortune 500* at the beginning of the period had dropped out by the end. By the late 1980s the rate had increased threefold (Newport, 1989). Even 'the best' have found the going tough, as evidenced by the fact that only 14 out of the 43 companies identified by Tom Peters and Robert Waterman's best-selling book *In Search of Excellence* were still regarded as 'excellent' less than 5 years later (Pascale, 1990). In the UK and elsewhere the picture has been no less dramatic. Meanwhile the early 1990s has seen spectacular corporate failures across the world.

While, on the one hand, these statistics illustrate the difficulties inherent in maintaining success, on the other, they point to the need for any organization to maintain a very high degree of awareness and capacity to learn in order to survive. Underlying this is the requirement to make decisions which are well informed. In the process, it also ensures that the organization's horizons are constantly being developed and extended.

The implications for training

Thus the process of adapting to the environment is not just an essential ingredient in the process of ensuring the future of an organization, it is also synonymous with continuous organization learning and development. In turn, this reflects the importance of, and provides the mechanism for, integrating management development with the continuous development of the entire workforce.

At both the general and specific levels, the problem for the trainer seeking to understand how changes in the environment will impact upon training needs lies in the fact that the variables are infinite and constantly changing. However, as a general starting point for analysis, it is worth considering a range of factors affecting the demand for and supply of skills. For example:

- *Increasing international competitiveness*: for most organizations and individuals this implies the attainment of ever higher standards of quality and efficiency. Underlying this is the need to acquire a broader outlook as well as work across boundaries, whether geographical or

organizational (for example, through cooperative ventures).
* *Technology and the rate of change*: is likely to continue to undermine the traditional bases of bureaucratic organization and mass production and the underlying principle of 'scientific management'. It also increases the importance of 'maintenance' skills, relative to those of 'direct production'.

For many businesses these factors imply the need for the continued shift to develop operational flexibility, the development of multi-skilled and interdisciplinary work teams and the acceptance by the individual of greater responsibility for the quality of their work.

* *Political developments*: these call for the ability to work with different and changing political and social systems and cultures, whether concerned, for example, with developments in the Single European Market, the shift in economic power to the Far East, political change in Eastern and Central Europe, the Middle East or Southern Africa, or the concentration of military power in the United States.
* *Social trends*: these include higher expectations regarding corporate governance, equal opportunities, health and safety and care for the environment. Common to them all is the requirement for greater levels of awareness and responsibility from members of the workforce in general and senior management in particular. Increasingly, also, concern is likely to have to be extended to those without work and for whom improved training is a prerequisite to obtaining employment and in order to maintain social cohesion and stability.
* *Demographic trends*: the ageing population in industrial economies affects both the demand for and supply of skills. For example, in terms of demand, an ageing population might be expected to borrow less and save more of its wealth, switching its pattern of consumption in the process. In terms of supply, these countries will have to rely on their older workers to stay on or return to work in order to avoid labour shortages. Within this, the participation rate of women in the workforce can be expected to continue, bringing their role into greater prominence.

In sharp contrast is the predicament resulting from the population explosion in the developing countries over the past forty years and which has led to a doubling of the world population. As George Kanawaty and Claudio de Moura Castro (1990) of the ILO put it:

The sheer size of the new generation of jobseekers in need of training is staggering. Their arrival on the labour market is already outstripping the capacity of existing institutions in many countries, and governments are finding it financially prohibitive to continue building new institutions to handle the increased numbers of the economically active (p.752).

They go on to explain how:

The temptation in these circumstances is to organize training for its own sake without much regard to the actual needs of the labour market and so perpetuate the same profile of trainees, irrespective of the changing patterns of demand for skills. Furthermore, there is a risk of the emphasis being placed almost exclusively on initial training to help trainees obtain a first job—with problems of upgrading and retraining for mobility left either to the enterprise, or to the individuals to resolve themselves later on—whereas today retraining, upgrading and life-long education needs are all increasingly important as a result of restructuring and changing technology.

It is within the context of these developments that organizations can begin to gauge the skills imbalances that face them. Although, by definition, specific needs will relate to the particular organization, in a general sense most businesses are likely to have to give high priority to developing their skills in a range of areas, simply to survive. Some of these are discussed below.

Quality

Although many organizations have made efforts to shift responsibility from 'quality controllers/departments' to line managers and work teams, few have successfully developed what could be described as total quality management (TQM). For this to be achieved, a real commitment from top management is required to ensure, for example:

- Acceptance of responsibility for quality throughout the organization
- Education and training of the workforce in the knowledge and use of appropriate tools and techniques of analysis
- Development of performance specifications in line with customer requirements and competitors' offerings
- Attitudes geared towards continuous improvement
- Adequate investment in training

Common to all of these aspects is the need for much greater awareness that TQM is a 'people' issue rather than a technical one.

Just-in-time working

Although generally seen in the context of production methods, Just-in-time (JIT) working affects and is capable of extension to all aspects of a business. As part of a competitive strategy it offers tremendous potential to improve both productivity, through better asset utilization, and levels of customer service.

The essence of JIT is that production is 'pulled' through the organization according to demand, rather than 'pushed' in accordance with rigid production schedules. Besides greater responsiveness to customer and market needs, the organization benefits from much-reduced levels of stocks and work in progress, reduced set-up times and improved utilization of the workforce.

By way of example, in retailing, JIT can lead to a much closer relationship between supplier and retailer to allow a quicker and more flexible response to fashion demands and seasonal variations. In the process, it reduces the risk in making buying decisions and the danger of being left with unsold stock (which would have to be sold at cut prices—

thereby reducing sales margins and cash flow, and limiting the ability to replace stocks with better selling lines).

To be effective, JIT requires major investment in training. Management needs highly developed skills of integration and the whole workforce must possess the attitude of mind and skills to switch quickly and willingly between tasks. In addition, employees generally need to be trained to higher skill levels in teamworking and in quality management so that, for example, they can both operate and maintain the production process and avoid lost time through machine breakdowns or raw material shortages.

Teamworking

The increasing use of teamwork reflects the greater awareness of the capacity of teams to make good use of a mix of abilities and experiences and, in particular, the scope they offer for providing adaptability and flexibility. They are of particular relevance where:

- Members have a shared goal
- Their work is interconnected and interdependent
- Members are (generally) responsible for organizing some, if not all, of the own work; completing it on time and to agreed quality standards; providing cover for their colleagues when absent or undergoing training; ensuring that members possess the necessary knowledge and skills to contribute to the work of the team

Within this framework it can be seen that working in teams calls for greater breadth of knowledge and skills than traditional methods, along with attitudes of mind consistent with greater maturity towards self-help, problem-solving and cooperation. It also calls for different skills of the team leader. Thus the role of 'supervision' is diminished and exchanged for that of leadership based on a helping and facilitating relationship.

Problem-solving skills

The faster the rate of change, the more essential is the need for organizations to possess problem-solving skills. Without them, there will not be the necessary improvements in levels of quality in products, support services, process development, cycle times and responsiveness which serve as the basis for improving customer satisfaction levels and remaining competitive.

At one level this calls for individuals to develop, as second nature and to a high standard, the disciplines of structured approaches to diagnosis and problem solving. (For a practical and helpful analysis and discussion of this, see Francis, 1990.) It is important to recognize that the acquisition of these skills is a rigorous and time-consuming process. Although, with experience, short cuts are possible, cutting corners tends to result in shallow and cosmetic solutions.

At another level, problem-solving calls for extended skills in order to make the best use of information technology. Riverso (1992, p.4) provides a simple example of this when he cites how IT can help in the area of telephony by enabling a company's telephone system to be connected to a database, so that when an employee answers the phone he or she can have a customer's details on the screen as they speak. The key point here is that IT will enable companies to treat customers as individuals—the first step in good service—and, in the process solve the problem of communications inherent in extending relationships with customers.

From a broader perspective IT is a means, provided users have been given the skills, to enabling cooperation between staff and the extension of the productivity gains from desktop personal computing to the whole organization. It also holds the key to the management of workflow. Besides the specific IT training requirements, both these developments carry implications for training in teamwork, since they involve a cultural shift away from that of the individual towards the organization as a whole. For a short but very readable review of this, see *Financial Times* (1992).

Organizational learning

Whether conscious or not, the capacity of an organization to be successful in developing and integrating these activities is likely to be dependent upon not just the level and quality of its investment in training but also its capacity to develop and manage organizational learning. It is also likely that organizations which have embraced such approaches as teamworking, total quality management and Just-in-time working will also have accepted the philosophy of organizational learning.

One of the most vivid illustrations of the nature and importance of this and its distinction from individual learning is provided by Argyris (1977) in his conception of 'double loop learning'. He achieves this by addressing the question as to the extent to which a thermostat possesses the capacity to learn. In doing so, he demonstrates how, through feedback, continuous change and learning become possible and people become 'alive' to the signals which point to individual growth and organizational development and success.

Fundamental to the success of the learning organization is the existence of interpersonal skills at all levels. Without them, the appropriate feed back mechanisms will not be in place, nor will there be sufficient openness and trust to engage in the learning process. For managers it also carries the implication that they need to be skilled in unlocking the talents of their staff and helping them learn how to learn and to accept responsibility for their personal development and continuous improvement of their performance.

Organizational learning also builds the bridge between continuous development and competence, for these aspects of learning can only be continuous if they are self-directed. If they are not, then the opportunity to learn from everyday experience cemented by formal training and development is lost. Likewise, the development of 'core competencies' and the conceptual foundation, which recognizes that the development of underlying abilities can be used in a whole range of different situations, can be a basis for providing training to a common standard for those who may possess very different experience.

Despite Argyris's seminal work, organizational learning is an area in which research remains in its infancy, yet it would seem now to be a philosophy whose time has come. The reason for this is that, as Christopher Lorenz (1992) puts it, a learning organization:

encourages continuous learning and knowledge generation at all levels; has processes which can move knowledge round the organization easily to where it is needed; and can translate that knowledge quickly into changes in the way the organization acts, both internally and externally.

Given the context in which organizations operate and the need to sustain competitive advantage, businesses would seem to have little choice as to whether or not they wish to embrace the philosophy—if they don't, they will fail. This point is well illustrated by Pascale (1990, pp.236–7) in his comparative study of General Motors, which he sees as 'struggling with its institutional metabolism' and Honda, 'thriving with the brisk heartbeat of a Seiko watch'. In the process he offers a useful framework of eight specific factors which influence an organization's capacity for learning:

1 The extent to which an elite group or single point of view dominates decision making
2 The extent to which employees are encouraged to challenge the status quo
3 The induction and socialization of newcomers
4 The extent to which data on performance, quality, consumer satisfaction, and competitiveness are cultivated or suppressed
5 The equity of the reward system and distribution of privilege
6 The degree of empowerment at all levels
7 The historical legacy and folklore
8 The integrity of contention management processes—particularly with respect to surfacing hard truths and confronting reality

However, it is important to recognize that such frameworks do not offer a panacea. Applied in piecemeal fashion or without proper commitment, they are more likely to result in sterility, cynicism and resentment, rather than vitality and effectiveness. Consistent with the theme running throughout this book, the crucial ingredients are the attitudes, knowledge and skills that underpin them and the extent to which they provide a climate of continuous learning and development in which people can grow.

References

Argyris, C. (1977) 'Double loop learning in organizations', *Harvard Business Review*, September-October.

Financial Times (1992) 'Software at Work: integrating the enterprise'.

Kanawaty, G. and C. Mouro Castro (1990) 'New directions for training: An agenda for action', *International Labour Review*, **129**, No.6.

Lorenz, C. (1992) 'Bending minds to a new learning cycle', *Financial Times*, 17 February: a review of Peter Senge's popular book: *The Fifth Discipline—The Art and Practice of the Learning Organization*, New York: Doubleday.

Newport Jr, J.P. (1989) 'A new era of rapid rise and ruin', *Fortune*, 24 April.

Pascale, R.T. (1990) *Managing on the Edge: how successful companies use conflict to stay ahead*, Harmondsworth: Viking.

Riverso, R. (1992) *1999 Now: a European Review*, IBM, Spring.

Conclusion to Part Six

At a time when the rate of change in the environment is ever increasing, the rapid adaptation and acquisition of skills can be seen to be the key to developing and sustaining competitive advantage. This affects all the members of a workforce in terms of their attitude and ability to:

- Keep abreast of developments
- Maintain and expand their knowledge
- Develop their skills
- Relate to and influence the environment.

To be effective, however, training plans need to relate to an organization as a whole. Only when carried out in this way can training serve as an integrating mechanism and basis for continuous organizational learning and development.

Questions to consider include:

What sorts of changes in the environment is your organization facing in the short, medium and longer terms?
What implications do these changes carry for the attitude, knowledge and skill needs of the workforce?
How can these needs best be met?
What resources has the organization got for meeting them?
What needs to be done next?

Appendix 1
Financial statements—
a note for trainers

In order to assess the financial structure performance and potential of an organization, trainers need to be able to do three things:

1 Understand financial statements
2 Understand the concepts of ratio analysis
3 Apply the techniques to their own situation

The intention here is to underpin Chapters 6, 7 and 10, which deal with the concepts and application of ratio analysis, by providing a brief and practical introduction to understanding accounts.

Discussion of accounting principle, concepts and conventions have been limited to the extent that they are necessary to provide such an understanding: this is not a text on accounting theory. If you need more, why not study a professional text, talk to your accountant or go on a course? In any event, enlisting the support of your accountant at an early stage as part of the process of assessing training needs has much to recommend it.

The relevance of financial statements

In the first place, what is required is a basic understanding of financial statements. Of particular importance are the balance sheet, the profit and loss account and the statement of sources and application of funds. In considering these statements it is important to be aware that they are composed of five main elements:

- Assets
- Liabilities
- Capital
- Revenues
- Expenses

These elements are all interrelated. Thus, profits accrue to capital and, in turn, revenues and expenses are sub-components of capital. Hence the profit and loss account provides a sub-analysis of the capital element of the balance sheet.

The balance sheet

The balance sheet is a snapshot of the assets and liabilities of a business at a particular point in time. Besides showing the sources of capital, it indicates how the resources are allocated and how much is owed by and to the business.

The assets side of the balance sheet generally shows two groups of assets—*fixed assets* and *current assets*.

Fixed assets are those which are held for long-term use in the business (for example, land and buildings, plant and equipment, fixtures and fittings, and vehicles). They also include intangible assets (for example, patents and goodwill). Unlike land and buildings, intangible assets do not have a physical existence, but nevertheless still have a value. Fixed assets are shown in the balance sheet at net book value, i.e. cost price, less a provision for depreciation to reflect the fact that assets wear out. It is important to note that depreciation, although a charge against profits, does not involve an outflow of cash. Nor does it mean that cash is necessarily available for the replacement of assets.

In some instances replacement costs may be considerably higher than the provision for depreciation has allowed for because of inflation or technical developments. This highlights the importance of skills in business planning. Some assets, land and buildings, for example, tend to appreciate over time. Accordingly, these may be shown at valuation, less any provision for depreciation.

Current assets are those which are used for carrying out business transactions (for example, stocks, debtors and cash). Under current assets, stocks may include raw materials, work in progress and finished goods. They are usually valued at cost, replacement cost or net realizable value, whichever is lowest. However, changes in costs may make stocks difficult to value. Yet the way stocks are valued directly affects profits—thus an increase or decrease in stock valuation of £1 million affects profits by the same amount. Inflation may result in stocks being undervalued and, as a result, profits being understated.

Debtors represent the sum of money owed to the business for goods and services already supplied but not yet paid for. It will include any provision for bad and doubtful debts charged in the Profit and Loss Account. Cash usually includes that in the bank as well as that in hand.

Liabilities include all amounts owed by the business. It can be helpful to regard them as external and internal. Thus external liabilities include current liabilities, i.e. amounts payable within one year (for example, trade creditors, bank overdraft and current tax) and longer-term liabilities (debentures, mortgages, long-term bank loans and hire-purchase loans). Internal liabilities consist of the capital invested in the business, i.e. the capital originally provided by the shareholders and accumulated reserves retained for use in the business and not distributed to shareholders in the form of dividends.

When examining a balance sheet it is always important to 'check the figures' in order to avoid misinterpretation. For example, in the case study in Chapter 10 it was noted that the underlying value of ABCO's land and buildings substantially exceeded that shown in the accounts. This provides an example of the difficulties and limitations inherent in the analysis of financial statements.

The real problem here lies with accounting practices which have resulted in balance sheets containing a mixture of costs and valuations. Underlying this are two opposing views on their function. Some insist that balance sheets are fundamentally a record of costs which, unlike those that go through the profit and loss accounts, are incurred for future benefits. Others look to balance sheets to provide an indication of value, hence the practice of showing tangible assets such as land and buildings at valuation rather than cost. Following this argument, they support the growing, albeit highly controversial, practice of revaluing intangible assets such as brand names.

In practice, focusing on costs may give a distorted view, particularly where they have been incurred at different points of time and added together. Equally, valuations may have been made according to different bases and which are incompatible. A further complication results from the growing use of off-balance sheet financing—accounting techniques which can conceal the extent of a company's borrowing and hence its financial position.

Particular attention needs to be given to the valuation of fixed assets of land and buildings. For example, their undervaluation might provide a false impression of the real return on capital being earned by the business, on the one hand, and its borrowing potential, on the other. As a result, differences and changes in methods of evaluating assets, the treatment of goodwill, the valuing of brands, calculating depreciation, capitalizing expenditure or writing it off against income, off-balance-sheet items and changing prices, etc. all point to the need to use a great deal of care in making comparisons and interpreting data.

From the trainer's point of view, business is primarily concerned with the adding of value. Therefore, in interpreting balance sheets trainers should be concerned about the extent to which they reflect values rather than costs. In this way, the trainer will also be seeking to understand important trends over a period of years as well as the current position. Providing appropriate care is taken to compare 'like with like', it should be possible to minimize the risks of serious misinterpretation.

The profit and loss account

One of the most important functions of accounting is to calculate the amount of profit—or loss—that a business has made. Whereas the balance sheet is concerned with the value of assets and liabilities at a particular point in time, the profit and loss account shows the results of trading over a period of time (for example, the previous year). It deals with sales, costs and profits.

When considering such statements it is important to understand that it is ultimately added value—i.e. sales less material costs—and not the volume of sales which determines the level of profits, since it is out of this amount that wages and expenses have to be paid. The significance of this for management and training policies should not be missed.

It is worth noting that the cost of materials is not the same as total purchases for the year. This is because a business holds stocks at the beginning of the year, purchased in the previous year but sold during this period. At the year-end the business holds closing stocks, bought this year but which will not be used until next. Hence the cost of materials used is calculated by adding the purchases for the year to opening stock and then deducting closing stock. Incidentally, this shows how the valuation of stocks affects the cost of sales figure and has a direct impact on profit calculations.

Statement of source and application of funds

The funds flow statement is important, for it shows the extent to which the business has been successful in generating additional funds, as distinct from profits, during the year, where they come from and how they have been applied.[1] Its particular value lies in the focus it provides on the cash flow generated by the business, on the extent to which working capital has grown or contracted and the consequential improvement or deterioration in liquidity. Thus, it reflects changes in the financial strength and standing of the business.

Funds are provided from two sources:

• An increase in a liability
• A decrease in an asset

Funds can be applied in two ways:

• A decrease in a liability
• An increase in an asset

Sources of funds are those items which increase working capital. They include pre-tax profit and adjustments for items not involving the movement of funds (for example, depreciation). This gives the total generated from operations.

Funds from other sources include sales of fixed assets, exchange adjustments and funds raised by issuing new shares or loan capital. These are then added to the total funds generated from other operations. The application of funds shows items which reduce working capital (for example, purchases of fixed assets and investments, payments of taxation and dividends, repayments of loans and overdrafts). Deducting the total for the application of funds from the total for sources of funds gives the net flow of funds. Changes in working capital are then shown, followed by net liquid funds.

When interpreting such statements, the trainer needs to give consideration to the following questions:

- How successful is the company at generating cash from its operations?
- Is internally generated cash flow sufficient to maintain and develop the business?
- To what extent is the company acquiring or disposing of fixed assets? Does this indicate expansion, renewal or decline?
- To what extent have fixed assets been financed from long- rather than short-term funds?
- To what extent is the company borrowing or raising additional capital? Is this for financial restructuring (for example, replacing one form of debt with another), or expansion?
- How is working capital changing? Are changes in levels of stocks and debtors offset by corresponding changes in creditors? Alternatively, does it seem that creditors are being used to finance trading by delaying payments to them, perhaps implying cash shortages? What does this suggest about the level of control?

Conclusion

The purpose of this brief introduction to financial statements has been to show how they can help the trainer get to grips with the business by forming a general view of its financial structure and results. In reviewing such statements, however, it needs to be borne in mind that:

1 It is important to check that the figures being used reflect the true position of the business. Where they do not, allowances and qualifications need to be made. The results for any given company could be very different using alternative accounting policies. It needs also to be remembered that those producing the accounts may be under considerable pressure to show the company in a favourable light.

2 Analysis based on balance sheet figures requires particular care since the figures are for one day only. This may mean, for example, that when calculating working capital ratios, a more accurate picture might be obtained by using average levels for stocks and debtors if they are available.

3 Inflation has an effect on the trends and profits of a business. Throughout this review the assumption has been made that accounts are prepared on the historical cost convention, i.e. that assets are shown at purchase price, less any write-offs. This can clearly be misleading, particularly in periods of high inflation, not least since for most businesses it results in a higher profit figure than would result from the adoption of current cost accounting.

4 The comparison of one business with another requires particular knowledge and care, because different methods may be used to value assets and calculate depreciation. Similarly, different policies will affect the capitalization or writing-off against income of expenditure on activities such as research and development.

5 International comparisons also require particular care, since accounting conventions and regulations can differ from one country to another.

6 Approaches to costing are arbitrary and it is therefore very important to assess the basis and quality of information. Analysis based on

defective information is likely to result in defective decisions!

7 Financial statements do not reflect all the strengths and weaknesses of a business. For example, except in very rare circumstances, no value is placed on its employees and their skills.

Provided that appropriate care is taken, the trainer will be able to begin to tune into the organization and its possible needs. In turn, this provides a sound basis and context for further investigation (for example, by conducting a more detailed financial analysis using the techniques of ratio analysis).

Note

1 In future, all medium and large companies in the UK with year-ends after 23 March 1992 will have to provide a cash flow statement in lieu of the old sources and application of funds statement. The new statement should be more revealing than hitherto and will make comparisons between companies much easier. It will also make comparisons with companies in the USA easier, since the formats will now be similar.

Appendix 2
Understanding the organization

Scope of the survey

The main subjects for review are those which reflect the organization's strategy and performance as a whole and its principal operating functions of the business. In looking at them, the trainer needs to gather information which will lead to an understanding of the organization's behaviour in order to identify the key areas where training can contribute to improving performance (for example, the better use of underused assets, and the more effective attainment of its goals). Thus the survey might be expected to cover the following:

1 Broad description of the organization
2 Context of the organization, i.e. its environment
3 Overall objectives, strategies, policies and plans
4 Functional operations, for example:
   —Marketing
   —Sales
   —Distribution
   —Research and development
   —Production and service
   —Finance
   —Purchasing
   —Stocks and materials
   —Personnel and training
5 Organization structure and culture

Organization overview

When, how, why and by whom was the business established?
How has the business developed and what have been the major events and features of this?
Where is it located?
What is its legal form and who are its main owners?
What are its principal activities, i.e. functions, products, markets?
How is it organized and structured?
How big is it in terms of revenue, volume and resources of capital, physical assets, productive capacity, personnel, technical and commercial knowhow? To what extent is quality reflected in these features?

What is the quality of earnings? For example, are profits dependent upon products and services where added value is minimal? Are they cyclical? Are they dependent upon reducing inventories, etc.?

Organizational context

What is the political climate and how does it impact upon the business?
What is the state of the economy and what are the likely major trends and developments within it?
What is the state of the markets and industry in which the organization operates?
What is the quality of the physical infrastructure, including, for example, communications and housing?
What is the availability of essential natural resources?
What is the availability of human resources? To what extent is it educated and trained to the needs of the business?
What is the state of the labour market and the likely trends within it?
What training facilities are available?
What socio-cultural factors need to be taken into account (for example, ethnic groupings and minorities, cultural and religious traditions)?
Which are the major trade union and employer federations involved and what influence do they have?
Which pressure groups might be concerned about the organization's activities?
What is the legal setting and how does it impact upon the organization, its employees and customers?

Overall objectives, policies, strategies and plans

What are the overall objectives of the organization, now and in the future?
What are the major areas in which objectives are set?
What major changes are planned (for example, overall performance, markets, product development, technology, and financial, physical and human resources)?
How are these plans to be achieved (for example, acquisition, diversification, divestment, or organization development)?
Are they explicit, measurable and indicative of performance requirements?
To what extent are they compatible or conflicting?
Do they reflect awareness and knowledge of the organization and its environment?
Are the objectives seen as realistic?
How do they relate to objectives and plans at lower levels of the organization?
How are they established, communicated and reviewed?
To what extent are they understood, accepted and acted upon?

Marketing

What is the role, function and importance of marketing in the organization?
How is it organized?

To what extent is there awareness of the size and structure of the market and important trends? Does it carry out or commission market research?

What is the organization's position in the market in terms of share and standing compared to its competitors?

Is there awareness of the major customers, actual and potential, and their needs?

How is it ensured that products and services are developed in line with customer needs and trends in the market?

How competitive is the organization in terms of quality, price, delivery and service?

What use is made of advertising and sales promotion? How is its effectiveness measured?

Sales

What is the size and structure of the sales force? What is its relationship to the customer base and organization?

How are targets set for maintaining existing business and developing new business?

How is performance measured and controlled? With what results?

Is there awareness of volume and revenue levels and trends, stock levels, selling expenses, sales profitability, lost orders, late deliveries, customer complaints?

What are the arrangements for recruitment, training, development and motivation? How effective are they?

Distribution

What is the distribution policy? How does it relate to the needs of customers, the sales force and production?

What are the warehousing and transport resources?

What are the systems for stock-holding levels and locations?

What are the arrangements for packing, despatch, routing and delivery?

How is stock loss, damage, deterioration, theft and other forms of wastage avoided?

How are operating efficiency standards and targets set, assessed and controlled?

Production and service

What is the role of production and service provision in the organization and what is the nature and quality of its relationships with other functions (for example, marketing, sales and distribution, research and development, purchasing, accounting and personnel)?

How is it organized and structured? What is its layout? What are the main material and product flows? What are its major strengths and how flexible is it?

What is the productive capacity and the level of utilization?

What is the technology involved and how does it compare to that of competitors?

What is the quality and condition of premises, plant and equipment?
What is the provision for the maintenance, depreciation and renewal of plant and equipment?
How is production planned and scheduled, coordinated and controlled? Is proper account taken of lead times?
What is the level and quality of support services (for example, industrial engineering, technical, work study, and quality control)?
How many production workers are employed? What are their principal skills and grades? What is their length of service and rate of turnover?
What payment systems are in operation and how are they supervised?
What is the quality and extent of induction, basic and continuous training provided?
What is the quality of the working environment? What are the arrangements for health and safety and how effective are they?
How is the quality and efficiency of production assessed? How are quality and productivity levels established and monitored?
What is the extent of lost time (for example, due to machine down-time, whether through breakdown, maintenance or setting, waiting for materials, accidents and absenteeism, etc.)? How is it monitored and controlled?
What are the levels of material wastage, scrap and rework? How are they recorded and dealt with?

Research and development

What is the status of research and development in the organization? How is it organized and funded?
Is there a research and development policy and is it translated into a strategy and plan?
What is the calibre of its staff and what are their major achievements?
What is the quality of facilities at their disposal? Are they supported by information services?
How is the success of the function measured?
To what extent have the needs of the organization for reduced production and service provision costs, the creation of new products and services, and improvements in products and service quality been met?

Finance

What is the role of the accounting and finance function in the organization? What are its policies?
Is the function appropriate to the size and nature of the organization?
What is the quality of its relationships with other functions and departments?
What is its structure and what are the different levels and grades of skill?
What is the quality and effectiveness of bookkeeping, recording and control systems?
Are helpful reports provided to assist in assessing progress and decision making?
To what extent do financial statements provide a 'true and fair view' of the organization's results and financial position?

Are reports provided reflecting, for example, overall and functional performance in financial terms, the effects of inflation or making comparisons with other organizations?

How effective is the system for recording costs and does it provide appropriate information to managers (for example, on direct and indirect costs and cost volume relationships, variance analysis)?

How are budgets prepared and integrated? How is responsibility allocated? How are they monitored and controlled? Do they result in the identification of areas for corrective action to be taken?

Do they possess the skills to contribute to investment decisions and the appraisal of capital projects?

To what extent is there awareness of the tax system and the potential implications for business decisions, for example:

- Income tax on the income of individuals
- Sales tax, value added tax and excise duties
- National Insurance contributions
- Corporate tax
- Capital gains tax
- Inheritance tax

Purchasing

What is the position of the function in the organization? How is it structured?

What is the proportion of expenditure on purchases as a percentage of total business expenditure?

How are purchasing specifications prepared? How frequently are they reviewed? Have they been published (for example, in the form of a directory)?

How are potential suppliers identified?

Have supplier profiles been developed? Do they include assessments of reliability?

How are order sizes determined?

What sort of training is provided in negotiation skills?

How is overall effectiveness defined and controlled?

Stocks and materials

Where does responsibility for the function lie? How is it organized?

How is the balance determined between meeting the needs of production, minimizing working capital requirements and ensuring the effective utilization of space? How successfully is it achieved?

How is the stores design and layout determined? How effective is it?

How are stock levels determined and controlled? How effective are they?

What is the level of stock-outs, losses, wastage and deterioration?

Personnel and training/human resources/ staffing

What is the position of the human resource function in the organization? Is it involved in shaping and articulating the human values of the organization?

What is its contribution to the long-term planning and development of the business, or is it seen primarily as a firefighting activity?

What is the quality of the relationship between personnel specialists and line management, employees and their representatives?

Are personnel staff involved in problem solving and development activities with line management?

To what extent have policies been developed for employee resourcing, training and development and industrial relations?

Do policies and practices reflect awareness of the business and its management, human resource strategies and techniques, and the social sciences?

What is the basis of human resource planning? Does it reflect awareness of trends in internal and external labour markets?

How is the effectiveness of recruitment and selection assessed? Are interviewers trained? Is appropriate use made of psychometric testing?

How effective is the system of staff appraisal?

What is the provision for training? How are needs assessed?

What are the arrangements and facilities for induction, basic and continuation training?

Have career structures been developed? To what extent do they reflect prospects?

Have the purpose and function of reward and payment systems been defined? How relevant are they in terms of attractiveness and optimizing group and individual performance?

Have industrial relations policies and procedural agreements been defined?

Are attitude surveys carried out to assess levels of employee satisfaction? What is their effect on the management and performance of the organization?

What is the quality of manpower information? Does it provide a picture of the organization in terms, for example, of:

- Age distributions
- Sex
- Ethnic origin
- Length of service
- Educational levels
- Occupational and skill groupings
- Levels of training and experience
- Transfers and promotions
- Remuneration
- Performance assessment
- Potential for development
- Establishment levels

How is this sort of information used? Does it contribute to improvements in performance and management decision making?
Are specific reports prepared to monitor and control labour turnover and stability, absence, sickness, accidents and disputes, etc.?
How is the function evaluated?

Structure

How is the organization structured overall and how has it evolved?
Is it characterized by centralization or decentralization?
Does its form tend to bureaucratic, market, matrix or other?
Does its form seem relevant to its purpose?
How are major functions, divisions, departments structured and coordinated? To what extent are they compatible? What are the implications arising from the differences?
What seem to be the informal communication channels and networks?
To what extent do these mirror the formal organization structures and mechanisms?

Key personnel

Who are the key managers and individuals?
What level of competence do they suggest, both individually and collectively?
What appear to be their personal goals within the organization?
What is the source, nature and extent of their power base?

Decision making

How are major decisions made? Is it primarily a collaborative or unilateral process? What happens when the going gets tough?
What is the balance between subjectivity and objectivity?
Are appropriate systematic and quantitative techniques used?
What is the quality of information available for decision making? How reliable is it? To what extent is it used?
In reaching decisions, what consideration is given to assessing counter-productive side effects?
How much openness is there to information which constitutes 'bad news' or is 'threatening'?
To what extent is the process influenced by the reward system (for example, financial, promotional and psychological), standard procedures, previous decisions, habit and threats to the status quo?
On balance, does the decision-making process seem likely to lead to the continuing survival of the organization or its demise?

Information systems and procedures

How clearly defined are system requirements?
How are needs determined and planned for?
Do systems and procedures provide sufficient information in terms of quantity and quality for overall management of the organization as well as functional activity and control?

What is the basic quality of the information system in terms of its technological base, cost effectiveness and impact on those who need to use it?

How are systems and procedures maintained and kept up to date?

Culture and style

What appear to be the fundamental values of the organization? How are they reflected in organization policies?

Do the values result in a cultural base which orientates the organization, for example, towards task accomplishment, bureaucratic control, personal power, individualism, etc.?

To what extent is this orientation consistent with the objectives of the organization and those who work in it?

Does it result in 'super-ordinate' goals to which employees can relate?

What is the process of socialization and how effective is it? To what extent is compliance a prerequisite for success (for example, promotion) and non-compliance a bar?

Is there a predominant management style? What is the balance between authoritarianism and individual responsibility? To what extent does it result in coercion and obedience, freedom and creativity—or anarchy?

Is the style consistent with the overriding culture? How are differences allowed for and managed?

Is the style consistent with the needs of the organization for flexibility and adaptability?

How does it relate to the wishes or needs of employees for involvement and development?

Bibliography

Alban Metcalfe, B. and N. Nicholson (1984) *The Career Development of British Managers*, London: British Institute of Management.

Allen, D. (1991) *Strategic Financial Management in Practice*, Financial Times Management Reports.

Argenti, J. (1976) *Corporate Collapse: the causes and symptoms*, New York: McGraw-Hill.

Argyle, M. (1978) *The Psychology of Interpersonal Behaviour*, 3rd edition, Harmondsworth: Penguin.

Argyris, C. (1977) 'Double loop learning in organizations', *Harvard Business Review*, September–October.

Business ratios: a new guide to interpretation, ICC.

Chandler Jr, A.D. (1962) *Strategy and Structure: Chapters in the History of American Industrial Enterprise*, Cambridge, MA: MIT Press.

Cooper, R. and R.S. Kaplan, (1988) 'Measure costs right: make the right decisions', *Harvard Business Review*, September–October, pp. 96–103.

Coulson, C. and T. Coe (1991) *The Flat Organisation: Philosophy and Practice*, London: British Institute of Management.

Davis, D. (1988) *How to Turn a Company Round: a practical guide to company rescue*, Cambridge: Director Books.

Deal, T.E. and A.A. Kennedy (1982) *Corporate Cultures: The Rites and Rituals of Corporate Life*, Reading, MA: Addison-Wesley.

Elliott, J. (1989) *Training Needs and Corporate Strategy*, IMS Report No 164, Institute of Manpower Studies.

Elliott, J. (1991) 'Training for profit—a review', *Transition*, January.

Financial Times (1992) 'Software at work: integrating the enterprise', Summer.

Financial Times (1992) 'The European Top 500'.

Fox, S., M. Tanton and S. McCleay (1992) *Human Resource Management, Corporate Strategy and Financial Performance*, The Management School, Lancaster University/ESRC, April.

Francis, D. (1990) *Effective Problem Solving*, London: Routledge.

Getting Paid. Justitia Unicol (1990) Harrow, Middx.

Greiner, L.E. (1972) 'Evolution and revolution as organizations grow', in *Harvard Business Review on Management*, July–August, p.41.

Handy, C. (1985) *Gods of Management*, London: Pan

Handy, C. (1989) *The Age of Unreason*, London: Business Books.

Harrison, R. (1972) 'How to describe your organization'.

Harvard Business Review, September–October.

Hersey, P. and K.H. Blanchard (1972) *Management of Organizational Behaviour*, Englewood Cliffs, NJ: Prentice Hall.

Investors in People: A Brief for Top Managers, Employment Department (1991).

Kanawaty, G. and C. Mouro Castro (1990) 'New directions for training: An agenda for action', *International Labour Review*, **129**, No.6.

Kanter, R.M. (1989) *When Giants Learn to Dance*, New York: Simon & Schuster.

Kubr, M. (ed.) (1986) *Management Consulting—A Guide to the Profession*, 2nd edition, Geneva: ILO.

Legge, K. (1978) *Power, Innovation, and Problem-solving in Personnel Management*, New York: McGraw-Hill.

Lewin, K. (1951) *Field Theory in Social Science*, New York: Harper and Row.

Lorenz, C. (1992) 'Bending minds to a new learning cycle', *Financial Times*, 17 February.

Management Policies and Practices, and Business Performance, a Report by the Centre for InterFirm Comparison, 1977.

Morgan, G. (1989) *Creative Organization Theory*, Beverly Hills, CA: Sage.

Newbould, G.D. and G.A. Luffman (1978) *Successful Business Policies*, Aldershot: Gower.

Newport Jr, J.P. (1989) 'A new era of rapid rise and ruin', *Fortune*, 24 April.

Parker, R.H. (1988) *Understanding Company Financial Statements*, 3rd edition, Harmondsworth: Penguin.

Pascale, R.T. (1990) *Managing on the Edge: how successful companies use conflict to stay ahead*, Harmondsworth: Viking.

Pendlebury, M.W. (ed.) (1989) *Management Accounting in the Public Sector*, London: Heinemann/CIMA.

Peppercorn, G. and G. Skoulding (1987) *Management Profile in British Industry*, London: British Institute of Management.

Performance Comparisons: Analysis of Key Financial Ratios, Lloyds Bowmaker (1989).

Peters, T.J. (1989) *Thriving on Chaos*, London: Pan.

Peters, T.J. and R.J. Waterman (1982) *In Search of Excellence*, New York: Harper & Row.

Porter, M.E. (1980) *Competitive Strategy: Techniques for Analyzing Industries and Competitors*, New York: The Free Press.

Porter, M.E. (1985) *Competitive Advantage*, New York: The Free Press.

Recruitment and Retention: Tackling the Universal Problem, IRS Employment Trends No. 447, 6 September 1989.

Reddin, W. (1988) *The Output-Oriented Organization*, Aldershot: Gower.

Revans, R.W. (1982) *The Origins and Growth of Action Learning*, London: Chartwell-Bratt, Chapter 45.

Riverso, R. 1992) *1999 Now: a European Review*, IBM, Spring.

Scapens, R.W. (1991) *Management Accounting: A Review of Recent Developments*, 2nd edition, London: Macmillan.

Senge, P. (1990) *The Fifth Discipline—The Art and Practice of the Learning Organization*, New York: Doubleday.

Skill Needs in Britain, Training Agency/IFF Research, 1990.

Sveiby, K.E. and T. Lloyd (1987) *Managing Knowhow*, London: Bloomsbury.

Taylor, B. (1984) 'Management training and development in the 1980's', in B. Taylor and G. Lippitt (eds), *The Management Development and Training Handbook*, 2nd edition, Maidenhead: McGraw-Hill.

Wheatley, M. (1991) *The Future of Middle Management*, London: British Institute of Management.

Index

Further titles in the McGraw-Hill Training Series

THE BUSINESS OF TRAINING
Achieving Success in Changing World Markets
Trevor Bentley   ISBN 0-07-707328-2

EVALUATING TRAINING EFFECTIVENESS
Translating Theory into Practice
Peter Bramley   ISBN 0-07-707331-2

DEVELOPING EFFECTIVE TRAINING SKILLS
Tony Pont   ISBN 0-07-707383-5

MAKING MANAGEMENT DEVELOPMENT WORK
Achieving Success in the Nineties
Charles Margerison   ISBN 0-07-707382-7

MANAGING PERSONAL LEARNING AND CHANGE
A Trainer's Guide
Neil Clark   ISBN 0-07-707344-4

HOW TO DESIGN EFFECTIVE TEXT-BASED OPEN
LEARNING:
A Modular Course
Nigel Harrison   ISBN 0-07-707355-X

HOW TO DESIGN EFFECTIVE COMPUTER BASED
TRAINING:
A Modular Course
Nigel Harrison   ISBN 0-07-707354-1

HOW TO SUCCEED IN EMPLOYEE DEVELOPMENT
Moving from Vision to Results
Ed Moorby   ISBN 0-07-707459-9

USING VIDEO IN TRAINING AND EDUCATION
Ashly Pinnington   ISBN 0-07-707384-3

TRANSACTIONAL ANALYSIS FOR TRAINERS
Julie Hay   ISBN 0-07-707470-X